Getting The Most From This Book

This book brings together a number of principles and practices that can help you with your mental health and general wellbeing. As with anything of this nature, it is important to engage with the content as much as possible to achieve the biggest benefits.

With that in mind though, it is important not to scold yourself for not completing a section or missing a few days. It should act as a means to concentrate the mind and give you a focus at the start and end of each day, helping to guide you and keep you focused on the things you want to be focused on, rather than the inevitable day to day distractions.

The page opposite is an important page. In those times when we need the most help, it is beneficial to have already listed out some things that can help you in those moments. Feel free to use these as work best for you - for example, if quotes just don't have any impact, substitute something that does. For the 'things and activities' this can be photographs, songs, mindfulness, swimming, reading etc absolutely anything that you find helpful. When you are next in a depressive state, reminding yourself of these things can be of great help.

The following page has a breakdown of each part of each entry type which will hopefully provide clarity as to the best way to approach them. These daily entries are split into two halves.

- Firstly, those that are to be completed first thing in the morning, ideally before you even look at your phone. By delaying looking at your phone, you begin the day on a solid footing based on your own wishes and desires. We also do not start the day by seeing some bad news, or something else on social media that has the ability to put us in a bad mood right from the off.

- Secondly, those that are to be completed later in the day, ideally at bedtime. This can help to clear the mind ready for bed and be part of a proactive bedtime routine that increases your chances of a good night sleep.

As stated above, if you skip one, or a day, or you don't achieve a goal etc, please do not worry about it. Nobody ever achieved all of their goals every day.

Science tells us that if we practise a new habit for 21 days straight, it begins to become part of our natural routine. So, whilst some of this may seem difficult to begin with, if you stick with it, it will become easier over time until it is a set part of your day.

I hope you find the book helpful and I hope you see a sustained improvement in your mental health.

 - Tom Wavre
Founder, iam1in4.com

www.iam1in4.com   Reducing the stigma around mental health

Example

Aim to complete the left hand side page first thing in the morning BEFORE you first check your phone or similar devices. Doing so helps to give you a solid base prior to the inevitable distractions of e-mail, social media, messages, news etc.

Approx how many hours did I sleep for?	How well rested am I?	Current Mood
Making such an estimate can be very hard. Please **DO NOT** clock watch as this is hugely counterproductive	1 = exhausted 6 = full of energy Don't overthink this, just give a gauge of how you are feeling, hopefully over time you will see an improvement	1 = awful 6 = amazing Don't overthink this, just give a gauge of your mood, hopefully over time you will see an improvement

My priorities today are...

By being sure what your priorities are for the day, you will be better able to maintain focus and keep a clear mind.

It is important that your listed priorities are fully achievable. Do not worry if they are small, like 'get out of bed'. Just keep them relevant to your situation.

No more than three, keep them realistic and do not berate yourself if you don't always achieve all three.

Fill in this section BEFORE you first check your phone, this will result in you being in control of your objectives and give you a good base for the day.

Today I am grateful for...

It has been proven that by expressing gratitude daily for 21 consecutive days you can begin to reprogramme your mind to look for the positives. This in turn improves your general mood and wellbeing.

These can be tiny, but try not to simply repeat the previous days list. It can include small things like being grateful for a glass of water, or a warm bed, a certain friend, your favourite band or tv show etc.

It may be hard at first, but maintaining this habit will be worth the effort in the long run.

www.iam1in4.com   Find us on Facebook, Twitter & Instagram

Evening

The right hand page can be completed at a time in the day that suits you best. However, it is recommended to make it part of your evening / bed time routine. By doing so you are able to put some of your concerns aside to help with a better night's sleep.

Journal Entry

Prompt for if you are struggling to know what to write: **How is your current mental health?**

Today I have:

Feel free to add your own examples
[ ] Exercised for 10 mins
[ ] Taken time to relax
[ ] Eaten well
[ ] Used my support network
[ ] Made my bed
[ ] Taken my medication
[ ] Connected with a friend
[ ] Disconnected from technology
[ ]
[ ]
[ ]

Tonight I am anxious about:

* Do not feel obliged to fill in anything here. The purpose is to put on paper anything that is troubling you as you attempt to sleep, doing so can often move the mind away from that thought.

www.iam1in4.com   Reducing the stigma around mental health

Morning

Aim to complete the left hand page first thing in the morning, BEFORE you first check your phone or similar devices. Doing so helps to give you a solid base prior to the inevitable distractions of e-mail, social media, messages, news etc.

Approx how many hours did I sleep for?	How well rested am I? 1 = exhausted 6 = full of energy	Current Mood 1 = awful 6 = amazing

My priorities today are...

1.

2.

3.

* Reminder: No more than 3, keep them realistic and do not berate yourself if you don't always achieve all 3.

Today I am grateful for...

1.

2.

3.

* Reminder: These can be tiny, but try to not simply repeat the previous day's list

www.iam1in4.com   Find us on Facebook, Twitter & Instagram

Evening

The right hand page can be completed at a time in the day that suits you best. However, it is recommended to make it part of your evening / bed time routine. By doing so you are able to put some of your concerns aside to help with a better night's sleep.

Journal Entry
Prompt for if you are struggling to know what to write: **Write about something good that happened this week**

Today I have:
Feel free to add your own examples
- [ ] exercised for 10 mins
- [ ] taken time to relax
- [ ] eaten well
- [ ] used my support network
- [ ] made my bed
- [ ] taken my medication
- [ ] connected with a friend
- [ ] disconnected from technology
- [ ]
- [ ]
- [ ]

Tonight I am anxious about:
*Do not feel obliged to fill in anything here. The purpose is to put on paper anything that is troubling you as you attempt to sleep, doing so can often move the mind away from that thought.

www.iam1in4.com   Reducing the stigma around mental health

Morning

Aim to complete the left hand page first thing in the morning, BEFORE you first check your phone or similar devices. Doing so helps to give you a solid base prior to the inevitable distractions of e-mail, social media, messages, news etc.

Approx how many hours did I sleep for?	How well rested am I? 1 = exhausted 6 = full of energy	Current Mood 1 = awful 6 = amazing

My priorities today are...

1.

2.

3.

* Reminder: No more than 3, keep them realistic and do not berate yourself if you don't always achieve all 3.

Today I am grateful for...

1.

2.

3.

* Reminder: These can be tiny, but try to not simply repeat the previous day's list

www.iam1in4.com   Find us on Facebook, Twitter & Instagram

Evening

The right hand page can be completed at a time in the day that suits you best.
However, it is recommended to make it part of your evening / bed time routine. By doing so you are able to put some of your concerns aside to help with a better night's sleep.

Journal Entry
* Prompt for if you are struggling to know what to write: What would you like to do over the next week?

Today I have:
Feel free to add your own examples
[ ] exercised for 10 mins
[ ] taken time to relax
[ ] eaten well
[ ] used my support network
[ ] made my bed
[ ] taken my medication
[ ] connected with a friend
[ ] disconnected from technology
[ ]
[ ]
[ ]

Tonight I am anxious about:
* Do not feel obliged to fill in anything here. The purpose is to put on paper anything that is troubling you as you attempt to sleep, doing so can often move the mind away from that thought.

www.iam1in4.com   Reducing the stigma around mental health

Morning

Aim to complete the left hand page first thing in the morning, BEFORE you first check your phone or similar devices. Doing so helps to give you a solid base prior to the inevitable distractions of e-mail, social media, messages, news etc.

Approx how many hours did I sleep for?	How well rested am I? 1 = exhausted 6 = full of energy	Current Mood 1 = awful 6 = amazing

My priorities today are...

1.

2.

3.

* Reminder: No more than 3, keep them realistic and do not berate yourself if you don't always achieve all 3.

Today I am grateful for...

1.

2.

3.

* Reminder: These can be tiny, but try to not simply repeat the previous day's list

www.iam1in4.com   Find us on Facebook, Twitter & Instagram

Evening

The right hand page can be completed at a time in the day that suits you best.
However, it is recommended to make it part of your evening / bed time routine. By doing so you are able to put some of your concerns aside to help with a better night's sleep.

Journal Entry
* Prompt for if you are struggling to know what to write: **What is one of your favourite memories?**

Today I have:
Feel free to add your own examples
[ ] exercised for 10 mins
[ ] taken time to relax
[ ] eaten well
[ ] used my support network
[ ] made my bed
[ ] taken my medication
[ ] connected with a friend
[ ] disconnected from technology
[ ]
[ ]
[ ]

Tonight I am anxious about:
* Do not feel obliged to fill in anything here. The purpose is to put on paper anything that is troubling you as you attempt to sleep, doing so can often move the mind away from that thought.

www.iam1in4.com Reducing the stigma around mental health

Morning

Aim to complete the left hand page first thing in the morning, BEFORE you first check your phone or similar devices. Doing so helps to give you a solid base prior to the inevitable distractions of e-mail, social media, messages, news etc.

Approx how many hours did I sleep for?	How well rested am I? 1 = exhausted 6 = full of energy	Current Mood 1 = awful 6 = amazing

My priorities today are...

1.

2.

3.

* Reminder: No more than 3, keep them realistic and do not berate yourself if you don't always achieve all 3.

Today I am grateful for...

1.

2.

3.

* Reminder: These can be tiny, but try to not simply repeat the previous day's list

www.iam1in4.com   Find us on Facebook, Twitter & Instagram

Evening

The right hand page can be completed at a time in the day that suits you best.
However, it is recommended to make it part of your evening / bed time routine. By doing so you are able to put some of your concerns aside to help with a better night's sleep.

Journal Entry
Prompt for if you are struggling to know what to write: **What can you learn from the last time you failed at something?**

Today I have:
Feel free to add your own examples
[ ] exercised for 10 mins
[ ] taken time to relax
[ ] eaten well
[ ] used my support network
[ ] made my bed
[ ] taken my medication
[ ] connected with a friend
[ ] disconnected from technology
[ ]
[ ]
[ ]

Tonight I am anxious about:
*Do not feel obliged to fill in anything here. The purpose is to put on paper anything that is troubling you as you attempt to sleep, doing so can often move the mind away from that thought.

www.iam1in4.com   Reducing the stigma around mental health

Morning

Aim to complete the left hand page first thing in the morning, BEFORE you first check your phone or similar devices. Doing so helps to give you a solid base prior to the inevitable distractions of e-mail, social media, messages, news etc.

Approx how many hours did I sleep for?	How well rested am I? 1 = exhausted 6 = full of energy	Current Mood 1 = awful 6 = amazing

My priorities today are...

1.

2.

3.

* Reminder: No more than 3, keep them realistic and do not berate yourself if you don't always achieve all 3.

Today I am grateful for...

1.

2.

3.

* Reminder: These can be tiny, but try to not simply repeat the previous day's list

www.iam1in4.com — Find us on Facebook, Twitter & Instagram

Evening

The right hand page can be completed at a time in the day that suits you best. However, it is recommended to make it part of your evening / bed time routine. By doing so you are able to put some of your concerns aside to help with a better night's sleep.

Journal Entry
* Prompt for if you are struggling to know what to write: **What makes you frustrated?**

Today I have:
Feel free to add your own examples
- [ ] exercised for 10 mins
- [ ] taken time to relax
- [ ] eaten well
- [ ] used my support network
- [ ] made my bed
- [ ] taken my medication
- [ ] connected with a friend
- [ ] disconnected from technology
- [ ]
- [ ]
- [ ]

Tonight I am anxious about:
* Do not feel obliged to fill in anything here. The purpose is to put on paper anything that is troubling you as you attempt to sleep, doing so can often move the mind away from that thought.

www.iam1in4.com   Reducing the stigma around mental health

Morning

Aim to complete the left hand page first thing in the morning, BEFORE you first check your phone or similar devices. Doing so helps to give you a solid base prior to the inevitable distractions of e-mail, social media, messages, news etc.

Approx how many hours did I sleep for?	How well rested am I? 1 = exhausted 6 = full of energy	Current Mood 1 = awful 6 = amazing

My priorities today are...

1.

2.

3.

* Reminder: No more than 3, keep them realistic and do not berate yourself if you don't always achieve all 3.

Today I am grateful for...

1.

2.

3.

* Reminder: These can be tiny, but try to not simply repeat the previous day's list

www.iam1in4.com   Find us on Facebook, Twitter & Instagram

Evening

The right hand page can be completed at a time in the day that suits you best. However, it is recommended to make it part of your evening / bed time routine. By doing so you are able to put some of your concerns aside to help with a better night's sleep.

Journal Entry
* Prompt for if you are struggling to know what to write: **What are your greatest strengths?**

Today I have:
Feel free to add your own examples
- [ ] exercised for 10 mins
- [ ] taken time to relax
- [ ] eaten well
- [ ] used my support network
- [ ] made my bed
- [ ] taken my medication
- [ ] connected with a friend
- [ ] disconnected from technology
- [ ]
- [ ]
- [ ]

Tonight I am anxious about:
* Do not feel obliged to fill in anything here. The purpose is to put on paper anything that is troubling you as you attempt to sleep, doing so can often move the mind away from that thought

Morning

Aim to complete the left hand page first thing in the morning, BEFORE you first check your phone or similar devices. Doing so helps to give you a solid base prior to the inevitable distractions of e-mail, social media, messages, news etc.

Approx how many hours did I sleep for?	How well rested am I? 1 = exhausted 6 = full of energy	Current Mood 1 = awful 6 = amazing

My priorities today are...

1.

2.

3.

* Reminder: No more than 3, keep them realistic and do not berate yourself if you don't always achieve all 3.

Today I am grateful for...

1.

2.

3.

* Reminder: These can be tiny, but try to not simply repeat the previous day's list

www.iam1in4.com   Find us on Facebook, Twitter & Instagram

Evening

The right hand page can be completed at a time in the day that suits you best.
However, it is recommended to make it part of your evening / bed time routine. By doing so you are able to put some of your concerns aside to help with a better night's sleep.

Journal Entry
* Prompt for if you are struggling to know what to write: **What really excites you?**

Today I have:
Feel free to add your own examples
- [ ] exercised for 10 mins
- [ ] taken time to relax
- [ ] eaten well
- [ ] used my support network
- [ ] made my bed
- [ ] taken my medication
- [ ] connected with a friend
- [ ] disconnected from technology
- [ ]
- [ ]
- [ ]

Tonight I am anxious about:
* Do not feel obliged to fill in anything here. The purpose is to put on paper anything that is troubling you as you attempt to sleep, doing so can often move the mind away from that thought.

www.iam1in4.com   Reducing the stigma around mental health

Morning

I am
1 in 4

Aim to complete the left hand page first thing in the morning, BEFORE you first check your phone or similar devices. Doing so helps to give you a solid base prior to the inevitable distractions of e-mail, social media, messages, news etc.

Approx how many hours did I sleep for?	How well rested am I? 1 = exhausted 6 = full of energy	Current Mood 1 = awful 6 = amazing

My priorities today are...

1.

2.

3.

* Reminder: No more than 3, keep them realistic and do not berate yourself if you don't always achieve all 3.

Today I am grateful for...

1.

2.

3.

* Reminder: These can be tiny, but try to not simply repeat the previous day's list

www.iam1in4.com   Find us on Facebook, Twitter & Instagram

Evening

The right hand page can be completed at a time in the day that suits you best.
However, it is recommended to make it part of your evening / bed time routine. By doing so you are able to put some of your concerns aside to help with a better night's sleep.

Journal Entry
* Prompt for if you are struggling to know what to write: **What have you learnt about yourself recently?**

Today I have:
Feel free to add your own examples
- [ ] exercised for 10 mins
- [ ] taken time to relax
- [ ] eaten well
- [ ] used my support network
- [ ] made my bed
- [ ] taken my medication
- [ ] connected with a friend
- [ ] disconnected from technology
- [ ]
- [ ]
- [ ]

Tonight I am anxious about:
* Do not feel obliged to fill in anything here. The purpose is to put on paper anything that is troubling you as you attempt to sleep, doing so can often move the mind away from that thought.

www.iam1in4.com   Reducing the stigma around mental health

Morning

Aim to complete the left hand page first thing in the morning, BEFORE you first check your phone or similar devices. Doing so helps to give you a solid base prior to the inevitable distractions of e-mail, social media, messages, news etc.

Approx how many hours did I sleep for?	How well rested am I? 1 = exhausted 6 = full of energy	Current Mood 1 = awful 6 = amazing

My priorities today are...

1.

2.

3.

* Reminder: No more than 3, keep them realistic and do not berate yourself if you don't always achieve all 3.

Today I am grateful for...

1.

2.

3.

* Reminder: These can be tiny, but try to not simply repeat the previous day's list

www.iam1in4.com   Find us on Facebook, Twitter & Instagram

Evening

The right hand page can be completed at a time in the day that suits you best.
However, it is recommended to make it part of your evening / bed time routine. By doing so you are able to put some of your concerns aside to help with a better night's sleep.

Journal Entry
* Prompt for if you are struggling to know what to write: **Write about a challenge you faced and overcame**

Today I have:
Feel free to add your own examples
[ ] exercised for 10 mins
[ ] taken time to relax
[ ] eaten well
[ ] used my support network
[ ] made my bed
[ ] taken my medication
[ ] connected with a friend
[ ] disconnected from technology
[ ]
[ ]
[ ]

Tonight I am anxious about:
* Do not feel obliged to fill in anything here. The purpose is to put on paper anything that is troubling you as you attempt to sleep, doing so can often move the mind away from that thought.

Morning

Aim to complete the left hand page first thing in the morning, BEFORE you first check your phone or similar devices. Doing so helps to give you a solid base prior to the inevitable distractions of e-mail, social media, messages, news etc.

Approx how many hours did I sleep for?	How well rested am I? 1 = exhausted 6 = full of energy	Current Mood 1 = awful 6 = amazing

My priorities today are...

1.

2.

3.

*Reminder: No more than 3, keep them realistic and do not berate yourself if you don't always achieve all 3.

Today I am grateful for...

1.

2.

3.

*Reminder: These can be tiny, but try to not simply repeat the previous day's list.

www.iam1in4.com   Find us on Facebook, Twitter & Instagram

Evening

The right hand page can be completed at a time in the day that suits you best.
However, it is recommended to make it part of your evening / bed time routine. By doing so you are able to put some of your concerns aside to help with a better night's sleep.

Journal Entry
* Prompt for if you are struggling to know what to write: **If you could meet one person, living or dead, who would it be and why?**

Today I have:
Feel free to add your own examples
- [ ] exercised for 10 mins
- [ ] taken time to relax
- [ ] eaten well
- [ ] used my support network
- [ ] made my bed
- [ ] taken my medication
- [ ] connected with a friend
- [ ] disconnected from technology
- [ ]
- [ ]
- [ ]

Tonight I am anxious about:
* Do not feel obliged to fill in anything here. The purpose is to put on paper anything that is troubling you as you attempt to sleep, doing so can often move the mind away from that thought.

www.iam1in4.com — Reducing the stigma around mental health

Morning

Aim to complete the left hand page first thing in the morning, BEFORE you first check your phone or similar devices. Doing so helps to give you a solid base prior to the inevitable distractions of e-mail, social media, messages, news etc.

Approx how many hours did I sleep for?	How well rested am I? 1 = exhausted 6 = full of energy	Current Mood 1 = awful 6 = amazing

My priorities today are...

1.

2.

3.

* Reminder: No more than 3, keep them realistic and do not berate yourself if you don't always achieve all 3.

Today I am grateful for...

1.

2.

3.

* Reminder: These can be tiny, but try to not simply repeat the previous day's list

www.iam1in4.com   Find us on Facebook, Twitter & Instagram

Evening

The right hand page can be completed at a time in the day that suits you best.
However, it is recommended to make it part of your evening / bed time routine. By doing so you are able to put some of your concerns aside to help with a better night's sleep.

Journal Entry
* Prompt for if you are struggling to know what to write: **Write a note to 'younger' you**

Today I have:
Feel free to add your own examples
- [ ] exercised for 10 mins
- [ ] taken time to relax
- [ ] eaten well
- [ ] used my support network
- [ ] made my bed
- [ ] taken my medication
- [ ] connected with a friend
- [ ] disconnected from technology
- [ ]
- [ ]
- [ ]

Tonight I am anxious about:
* Do not feel obliged to fill in anything here. The purpose is to put on paper anything that is troubling you as you attempt to sleep, doing so can often move the mind away from that thought.

www.iam1in4.com   Reducing the stigma around mental health

Morning

Aim to complete the left hand page first thing in the morning, BEFORE you first check your phone or similar devices. Doing so helps to give you a solid base prior to the inevitable distractions of e-mail, social media, messages, news etc.

Approx how many hours did I sleep for?	How well rested am I? 1 = exhausted 6 = full of energy	Current Mood 1 = awful 6 = amazing

My priorities today are...

1.

2.

3.

* Reminder: No more than 3, keep them realistic and do not berate yourself if you don't always achieve all 3.

Today I am grateful for...

1.

2.

3.

* Reminder: These can be tiny, but try to not simply repeat the previous day's list

www.iam1in4.com   Find us on Facebook, Twitter & Instagram

Evening

The right hand page can be completed at a time in the day that suits you best.
However, it is recommended to make it part of your evening / bed time routine. By doing so you are able to put some of your concerns aside to help with a better night's sleep.

Journal Entry
* Prompt for if you are struggling to know what to write: **Write a note to 'future' you**

Today I have:
Feel free to add your own examples
- [ ] exercised for 10 mins
- [ ] taken time to relax
- [ ] eaten well
- [ ] used my support network
- [ ] made my bed
- [ ] taken my medication
- [ ] connected with a friend
- [ ] disconnected from technology
- [ ]
- [ ]
- [ ]

Tonight I am anxious about:
* Do not feel obliged to fill in anything here. The purpose is to put on paper anything that is troubling you as you attempt to sleep, doing so can often move the mind away from that thought.

www.iam1in4.com   Reducing the stigma around mental health

Morning

Aim to complete the left hand page first thing in the morning, BEFORE you first check your phone or similar devices. Doing so helps to give you a solid base prior to the inevitable distractions of e-mail, social media, messages, news etc.

Approx how many hours did I sleep for?	How well rested am I? 1 = exhausted 6 = full of energy	Current Mood 1 = awful 6 = amazing

My priorities today are...

1.

2.

3.

* Reminder: No more than 3, keep them realistic and do not berate yourself if you don't always achieve all 3.

Today I am grateful for...

1.

2.

3.

* Reminder: These can be tiny, but try to not simply repeat the previous day's list

www.iam1in4.com   Find us on Facebook, Twitter & Instagram

Evening

The right hand page can be completed at a time in the day that suits you best.
However, it is recommended to make it part of your evening / bed time routine. By doing so you are able to put some of your concerns aside to help with a better night's sleep.

Journal Entry
* Prompt for if you are struggling to know what to write: **What would you do if you didn't have any fears?**

Today I have:
Feel free to add your own examples
[ ] exercised for 10 mins
[ ] taken time to relax
[ ] eaten well
[ ] used my support network
[ ] made my bed
[ ] taken my medication
[ ] connected with a friend
[ ] disconnected from technology
[ ]
[ ]
[ ]

Tonight I am anxious about:
* Do not feel obliged to fill in anything here. The purpose is to put on paper anything that is troubling you as you attempt to sleep, doing so can often move the mind away from that thought.

I am
1 in 4

Morning

Aim to complete the left hand page first thing in the morning, BEFORE you first check your phone or similar devices. Doing so helps to give you a solid base prior to the inevitable distractions of e-mail, social media, messages, news etc.

Approx how many hours did I sleep for?	How well rested am I? 1 = exhausted 6 = full of energy	Current Mood 1 = awful 6 = amazing

My priorities today are...

1.

2.

3.

* Reminder: No more than 3, keep them realistic and do not berate yourself if you don't always achieve all 3.

Today I am grateful for...

1.

2.

3.

* Reminder: These can be tiny, but try to not simply repeat the previous day's list

www.iam1in4.com   Find us on Facebook, Twitter & Instagram

Evening

The right hand page can be completed at a time in the day that suits you best.
However, it is recommended to make it part of your evening / bed time routine. By doing so you are able to put some of your concerns aside to help with a better night's sleep.

Journal Entry
Prompt for if you are struggling to know what to write: **What have you read recently that really made you think?**

Today I have:
Feel free to add your own examples
[ ] exercised for 10 mins
[ ] taken time to relax
[ ] eaten well
[ ] used my support network
[ ] made my bed
[ ] taken my medication
[ ] connected with a friend
[ ] disconnected from technology
[ ]
[ ]
[ ]

Tonight I am anxious about:
* Do not feel obliged to fill in anything here. The purpose is to put on paper anything that is troubling you as you attempt to sleep, doing so can often move the mind away from that thought.

www.iam1in4.com   Reducing the stigma around mental health

Morning

Aim to complete the left hand page first thing in the morning, BEFORE you first check your phone or similar devices. Doing so helps to give you a solid base prior to the inevitable distractions of e-mail, social media, messages, news etc.

Approx how many hours did I sleep for?	How well rested am I? 1 = exhausted 6 = full of energy	Current Mood 1 = awful 6 = amazing

My priorities today are...

1.

2.

3.

* Reminder: No more than 3, keep them realistic and do not berate yourself if you don't always achieve all 3.

Today I am grateful for...

1.

2.

3.

* Reminder: These can be tiny, but try to not simply repeat the previous day's list

www.iam1in4.com   Find us on Facebook, Twitter & Instagram

Evening

The right hand page can be completed at a time in the day that suits you best.
However, it is recommended to make it part of your evening / bed time routine. By doing so you are able to put some of your concerns aside to help with a better night's sleep.

Journal Entry
* Prompt for if you are struggling to know what to write: **If you remember one thing from today, what do you want it to be?**

Today I have:
Feel free to add your own examples

[ ] exercised for 10 mins
[ ] taken time to relax
[ ] eaten well
[ ] used my support network
[ ] made my bed
[ ] taken my medication
[ ] connected with a friend
[ ] disconnected from technology
[ ]
[ ]
[ ]

Tonight I am anxious about:
* Do not feel obliged to fill in anything here. The purpose is to put on paper anything that is troubling you as you attempt to sleep, doing so can often move the mind away from that thought.

Morning

Aim to complete the left hand page first thing in the morning, BEFORE you first check your phone or similar devices. Doing so helps to give you a solid base prior to the inevitable distractions of e-mail, social media, messages, news etc.

Approx how many hours did I sleep for?	How well rested am I? 1 = exhausted 6 = full of energy	Current Mood 1 = awful 6 = amazing

My priorities today are...

1.

2.

3.

* Reminder: No more than 3, keep them realistic and do not berate yourself if you don't always achieve all 3.

Today I am grateful for...

1.

2.

3.

* Reminder: These can be tiny, but try to not simply repeat the previous day's list

www.iam1in4.com   Find us on Facebook, Twitter & Instagram

Evening

The right hand page can be completed at a time in the day that suits you best. However, it is recommended to make it part of your evening / bed time routine. By doing so you are able to put some of your concerns aside to help with a better night's sleep.

Journal Entry
* Prompt for if you are struggling to know what to write: **What things always help you feel a little better?**

Today I have:
Feel free to add your own examples
[ ] exercised for 10 mins
[ ] taken time to relax
[ ] eaten well
[ ] used my support network
[ ] made my bed
[ ] taken my medication
[ ] connected with a friend
[ ] disconnected from technology
[ ]
[ ]
[ ]

Tonight I am anxious about:
* Do not feel obliged to fill in anything here. The purpose is to put on paper anything that is troubling you as you attempt to sleep, doing so can often move the mind away from that thought.

www.iam1in4.com — Reducing the stigma around mental health

Morning

Aim to complete the left hand page first thing in the morning, BEFORE you first check your phone or similar devices. Doing so helps to give you a solid base prior to the inevitable distractions of e-mail, social media, messages, news etc.

Approx how many hours did I sleep for?	How well rested am I? 1 = exhausted 6 = full of energy	Current Mood 1 = awful 6 = amazing

My priorities today are...

1.

2.

3.

* Reminder: No more than 3, keep them realistic and do not berate yourself if you don't always achieve all 3.

Today I am grateful for...

1.

2.

3.

* Reminder: These can be tiny, but try to not simply repeat the previous day's list

www.iam1in4.com   Find us on Facebook, Twitter & Instagram

Evening

The right hand page can be completed at a time in the day that suits you best.
However, it is recommended to make it part of your evening / bed time routine. By doing so you are able to put some of your concerns aside to help with a better night's sleep.

Journal Entry
* Prompt for if you are struggling to know what to write: **What do you wish people knew about you?**

Today I have:
Feel free to add your own examples
- [ ] exercised for 10 mins
- [ ] taken time to relax
- [ ] eaten well
- [ ] used my support network
- [ ] made my bed
- [ ] taken my medication
- [ ] connected with a friend
- [ ] disconnected from technology
- [ ]
- [ ]
- [ ]

Tonight I am anxious about:
* Do not feel obliged to fill in anything here. The purpose is to put on paper anything that is troubling you as you attempt to sleep, doing so can often move the mind away from that thought.

www.iam1in4.com   Reducing the stigma around mental health

Morning

Aim to complete the left hand page first thing in the morning, BEFORE you first check your phone or similar devices. Doing so helps to give you a solid base prior to the inevitable distractions of e-mail, social media, messages, news etc.

Approx how many hours did I sleep for?	How well rested am I? 1 = exhausted 6 = full of energy	Current Mood 1 = awful 6 = amazing

My priorities today are…

1.

2.

3.

*Reminder: No more than 3, keep them realistic and do not berate yourself if you don't always achieve all 3.

Today I am grateful for…

1.

2.

3.

*Reminder: These can be tiny, but try to not simply repeat the previous day's list

www.iam1in4.com   Find us on Facebook, Twitter & Instagram

Evening

The right hand page can be completed at a time in the day that suits you best.
However, it is recommended to make it part of your evening / bed time routine. By doing so you are able to put some of your concerns aside to help with a better night's sleep.

Journal Entry
* Prompt for if you are struggling to know what to write: **What is your favourite guilty pleasure?**

Today I have:
Feel free to add your own examples
- [ ] exercised for 10 mins
- [ ] taken time to relax
- [ ] eaten well
- [ ] used my support network
- [ ] made my bed
- [ ] taken my medication
- [ ] connected with a friend
- [ ] disconnected from technology
- [ ]
- [ ]
- [ ]

Tonight I am anxious about:
* Do not feel obliged to fill in anything here. The purpose is to put on paper anything that is troubling you as you attempt to sleep, doing so can often move the mind away from that thought.

www.iam1in4.com   Reducing the stigma around mental health

Morning

Aim to complete the left hand page first thing in the morning, BEFORE you first check your phone or similar devices. Doing so helps to give you a solid base prior to the inevitable distractions of e-mail, social media, messages, news etc.

Approx how many hours did I sleep for?	How well rested am I? 1 = exhausted 6 = full of energy	Current Mood 1 = awful 6 = amazing

My priorities today are...

1.

2.

3.

*Reminder: No more than 3, keep them realistic and do not berate yourself if you don't always achieve all 3.

Today I am grateful for...

1.

2.

3.

*Reminder: These can be tiny, but try to not simply repeat the previous day's list

www.iam1in4.com   Find us on Facebook, Twitter & Instagram

Evening

The right hand page can be completed at a time in the day that suits you best. However, it is recommended to make it part of your evening / bed time routine. By doing so you are able to put some of your concerns aside to help with a better night's sleep.

Journal Entry
* Prompt for if you are struggling to know what to write: **What is something you want to learn more about and how would you go about doing so**

Today I have:
Feel free to add your own examples
[ ] exercised for 10 mins
[ ] taken time to relax
[ ] eaten well
[ ] used my support network
[ ] made my bed
[ ] taken my medication
[ ] connected with a friend
[ ] disconnected from technology
[ ]
[ ]
[ ]

Tonight I am anxious about:
* Do not feel obliged to fill in anything here. The purpose is to put on paper anything that is troubling you as you attempt to sleep, doing so can often move the mind away from that thought.

www.iam1in4.com   Reducing the stigma around mental health

Morning

Aim to complete the left hand page first thing in the morning, BEFORE you first check your phone or similar devices. Doing so helps to give you a solid base prior to the inevitable distractions of e-mail, social media, messages, news etc.

Approx how many hours did I sleep for?	How well rested am I? 1 = exhausted 6 = full of energy	Current Mood 1 = awful 6 = amazing

My priorities today are...

1.

2.

3.

* Reminder: No more than 3, keep them realistic and do not berate yourself if you don't always achieve all 3.

Today I am grateful for...

1.

2.

3.

* Reminder: These can be tiny, but try to not simply repeat the previous day's list

www.iam1in4.com   Find us on Facebook, Twitter & Instagram

Evening

The right hand page can be completed at a time in the day that suits you best.
However, it is recommended to make it part of your evening / bed time routine. By doing so you are able to put some of your concerns aside to help with a better night's sleep.

Journal Entry
* Prompt for if you are struggling to know what to write: **What are you most afraid of, and why?**

Today I have:
Feel free to add your own examples
- [ ] exercised for 10 mins
- [ ] taken time to relax
- [ ] eaten well
- [ ] used my support network
- [ ] made my bed
- [ ] taken my medication
- [ ] connected with a friend
- [ ] disconnected from technology
- [ ]
- [ ]
- [ ]

Tonight I am anxious about:
* Do not feel obliged to fill in anything here. The purpose is to put on paper anything that is troubling you as you attempt to sleep, doing so can often move the mind away from that thought

www.iam1in4.com   Reducing the stigma around mental health

Morning

Aim to complete the left hand page first thing in the morning, BEFORE you first check your phone or similar devices. Doing so helps to give you a solid base prior to the inevitable distractions of e-mail, social media, messages, news etc.

Approx how many hours did I sleep for?	How well rested am I? 1 = exhausted 6 = full of energy	Current Mood 1 = awful 6 = amazing

My priorities today are...

1.

2.

3.

* Reminder: No more than 3, keep them realistic and do not berate yourself if you don't always achieve all 3.

Today I am grateful for...

1.

2.

3.

* Reminder: These can be tiny, but try to not simply repeat the previous day's list

www.iam1in4.com   Find us on Facebook, Twitter & Instagram

Evening

The right hand page can be completed at a time in the day that suits you best.
However, it is recommended to make it part of your evening / bed time routine. By doing so you are able to put some of your concerns aside to help with a better night's sleep.

Journal Entry
* Prompt for if you are struggling to know what to write: **What can you proactively do to benefit your mental health**

Today I have:
Feel free to add your own examples
[ ] exercised for 10 mins
[ ] taken time to relax
[ ] eaten well
[ ] used my support network
[ ] made my bed
[ ] taken my medication
[ ] connected with a friend
[ ] disconnected from technology
[ ]
[ ]
[ ]

Tonight I am anxious about:
* Do not feel obliged to fill in anything here. The purpose is to put on paper anything that is troubling you as you attempt to sleep, doing so can often move the mind away from that thought.

www.iam1in4.com   Reducing the stigma around mental health

Morning

Aim to complete the left hand page first thing in the morning, BEFORE you first check your phone or similar devices. Doing so helps to give you a solid base prior to the inevitable distractions of e-mail, social media, messages, news etc.

Approx how many hours did I sleep for?	How well rested am I? 1 = exhausted 6 = full of energy	Current Mood 1 = awful 6 = amazing

My priorities today are...

1.

2.

3.

*Reminder: No more than 3, keep them realistic and do not berate yourself if you don't always achieve all 3.

Today I am grateful for...

1.

2.

3.

*Reminder: These can be tiny, but try to not simply repeat the previous day's list.

www.iam1in4.com   Find us on Facebook, Twitter & Instagram

Evening

The right hand page can be completed at a time in the day that suits you best.
However, it is recommended to make it part of your evening / bed time routine. By doing so you are able to put some of your concerns aside to help with a better night's sleep.

Journal Entry
* Prompt for if you are struggling to know what to write: Who would you want to say thank you to and why?

Today I have:
Feel free to add your own examples
[ ] exercised for 10 mins
[ ] taken time to relax
[ ] eaten well
[ ] used my support network
[ ] made my bed
[ ] taken my medication
[ ] connected with a friend
[ ] disconnected from technology
[ ]
[ ]
[ ]

Tonight I am anxious about:
* Do not feel obliged to fill in anything here. The purpose is to put on paper anything that is troubling you as you attempt to sleep, doing so can often move the mind away from that thought.

www.iam1in4.com — Reducing the stigma around mental health

Morning

Aim to complete the left hand page first thing in the morning, BEFORE you first check your phone or similar devices. Doing so helps to give you a solid base prior to the inevitable distractions of e-mail, social media, messages, news etc.

Approx how many hours did I sleep for?	How well rested am I? 1 = exhausted 6 = full of energy	Current Mood 1 = awful 6 = amazing

My priorities today are...

1.

2.

3.

* Reminder: No more than 3, keep them realistic and do not berate yourself if you don't always achieve all 3.

Today I am grateful for...

1.

2.

3.

* Reminder: These can be tiny, but try to not simply repeat the previous day's list

www.iam1in4.com   Find us on Facebook, Twitter & Instagram

Evening

The right hand page can be completed at a time in the day that suits you best.
However, it is recommended to make it part of your evening / bed time routine. By doing so you are able to put some of your concerns aside to help with a better night's sleep.

Journal Entry
* Prompt for if you are struggling to know what to write: What do you want to be better at, how would you go about improving in that area?

Today I have:
Feel free to add your own examples
[ ] exercised for 10 mins
[ ] taken time to relax
[ ] eaten well
[ ] used my support network
[ ] made my bed
[ ] taken my medication
[ ] connected with a friend
[ ] disconnected from technology
[ ]
[ ]
[ ]

Tonight I am anxious about:
* Do not feel obliged to fill in anything here. The purpose is to put on paper anything that is troubling you as you attempt to sleep, doing so can often move the mind away from that thought.

www.iam1in4.com   Reducing the stigma around mental health

Morning

Aim to complete the left hand page first thing in the morning, BEFORE you first check your phone or similar devices. Doing so helps to give you a solid base prior to the inevitable distractions of e-mail, social media, messages, news etc.

Approx how many hours did I sleep for?	How well rested am I? 1 = exhausted 6 = full of energy	Current Mood 1 = awful 6 = amazing

My priorities today are...

1.

2.

3.

* Reminder: No more than 3, keep them realistic and do not berate yourself if you don't always achieve all 3.

Today I am grateful for...

1.

2.

3.

* Reminder: These can be tiny, but try to not simply repeat the previous day's list

www.iam1in4.com   Find us on Facebook, Twitter & Instagram

Evening

The right hand page can be completed at a time in the day that suits you best.
However, it is recommended to make it part of your evening / bed time routine. By doing so you are able to put some of your concerns aside to help with a better night's sleep.

Journal Entry
* Prompt for if you are struggling to know what to write: **Describe your happiest childhood memory**

Today I have:
Feel free to add your own examples
[ ] exercised for 10 mins
[ ] taken time to relax
[ ] eaten well
[ ] used my support network
[ ] made my bed
[ ] taken my medication
[ ] connected with a friend
[ ] disconnected from technology
[ ]
[ ]
[ ]

Tonight I am anxious about:
* Do not feel obliged to fill in anything here. The purpose is to put on paper anything that is troubling you as you attempt to sleep, doing so can often move the mind away from that thought.

www.iam1in4.com   Reducing the stigma around mental health

Morning

Aim to complete the left hand page first thing in the morning, BEFORE you first check your phone or similar devices. Doing so helps to give you a solid base prior to the inevitable distractions of e-mail, social media, messages, news etc.

Approx how many hours did I sleep for?	How well rested am I? 1 = exhausted 6 = full of energy	Current Mood 1 = awful 6 = amazing

My priorities today are...

1.

2.

3.

* Reminder: No more than 3, keep them realistic and do not berate yourself if you don't always achieve all 3.

Today I am grateful for...

1.

2.

3.

* Reminder: These can be tiny, but try to not simply repeat the previous day's list

www.iam1in4.com   Find us on Facebook, Twitter & Instagram

Evening

The right hand page can be completed at a time in the day that suits you best.
However, it is recommended to make it part of your evening / bed time routine. By doing so you are able to put some of your concerns aside to help with a better night's sleep.

Journal Entry
* Prompt for if you are struggling to know what to write: **What do you want to remember when you are struggling?**

Today I have:
Feel free to add your own examples
[ ] exercised for 10 mins
[ ] taken time to relax
[ ] eaten well
[ ] used my support network
[ ] made my bed
[ ] taken my medication
[ ] connected with a friend
[ ] disconnected from technology
[ ]
[ ]
[ ]

Tonight I am anxious about:
* Do not feel obliged to fill in anything here. The purpose is to put on paper anything that is troubling you as you attempt to sleep, doing so can often move the mind away from that thought.

Morning

Aim to complete the left hand page first thing in the morning, BEFORE you first check your phone or similar devices. Doing so helps to give you a solid base prior to the inevitable distractions of e-mail, social media, messages, news etc.

Approx how many hours did I sleep for?	How well rested am I? 1 = exhausted 6 = full of energy	Current Mood 1 = awful 6 = amazing

My priorities today are...

1.

2.

3.

* Reminder: No more than 3, keep them realistic and do not berate yourself if you don't always achieve all 3.

Today I am grateful for...

1.

2.

3.

* Reminder: These can be tiny, but try to not simply repeat the previous day's list

www.iam1in4.com   Find us on Facebook, Twitter & Instagram

Evening

The right hand page can be completed at a time in the day that suits you best.
However, it is recommended to make it part of your evening / bed time routine. By doing so you are able to put some of your concerns aside to help with a better night's sleep.

Journal Entry
* Prompt for if you are struggling to know what to write: **What do you want to achieve in life?**

Today I have:
Feel free to add your own examples
- [ ] exercised for 10 mins
- [ ] taken time to relax
- [ ] eaten well
- [ ] used my support network
- [ ] made my bed
- [ ] taken my medication
- [ ] connected with a friend
- [ ] disconnected from technology
- [ ]
- [ ]
- [ ]

Tonight I am anxious about:
* Do not feel obliged to fill in anything here. The purpose is to put on paper anything that is troubling you as you attempt to sleep, doing so can often move the mind away from that thought.

www.iam1in4.com   Reducing the stigma around mental health

Morning

Aim to complete the left hand page first thing in the morning, BEFORE you first check your phone or similar devices. Doing so helps to give you a solid base prior to the inevitable distractions of e-mail, social media, messages, news etc.

Approx how many hours did I sleep for?	How well rested am I? 1 = exhausted 6 = full of energy	Current Mood 1 = awful 6 = amazing

My priorities today are...

1.

2.

3.

* Reminder: No more than 3, keep them realistic and do not berate yourself if you don't always achieve all 3.

Today I am grateful for...

1.

2.

3.

* Reminder: These can be tiny, but try to not simply repeat the previous day's list

www.iam1in4.com   Find us on Facebook, Twitter & Instagram

Evening

The right hand page can be completed at a time in the day that suits you best.
However, it is recommended to make it part of your evening / bed time routine. By doing so you are able to put some of your concerns aside to help with a better night's sleep.

Journal Entry
* Prompt for if you are struggling to know what to write: **What is one place in the world you want to visit?**

Today I have:
Feel free to add your own examples
- [ ] exercised for 10 mins
- [ ] taken time to relax
- [ ] eaten well
- [ ] used my support network
- [ ] made my bed
- [ ] taken my medication
- [ ] connected with a friend
- [ ] disconnected from technology
- [ ]
- [ ]
- [ ]

Tonight I am anxious about:
* Do not feel obliged to fill in anything here. The purpose is to put on paper anything that is troubling you as you attempt to sleep, doing so can often move the mind away from that thought.

www.iam1in4.com   Reducing the stigma around mental health

Morning

Aim to complete the left hand page first thing in the morning, BEFORE you first check your phone or similar devices. Doing so helps to give you a solid base prior to the inevitable distractions of e-mail, social media, messages, news etc.

Approx how many hours did I sleep for?	How well rested am I? 1 = exhausted 6 = full of energy	Current Mood 1 = awful 6 = amazing

My priorities today are...

1.

2.

3.

* Reminder: No more than 3, keep them realistic and do not berate yourself if you don't always achieve all 3.

Today I am grateful for...

1.

2.

3.

* Reminder: These can be tiny, but try to not simply repeat the previous day's list

www.iam1in4.com　　　　　　　　　　Find us on Facebook, Twitter & Instagram

Evening

The right hand page can be completed at a time in the day that suits you best.
However, it is recommended to make it part of your evening / bed time routine. By doing so you are able to put some of your concerns aside to help with a better night's sleep.

Journal Entry
* Prompt for if you are struggling to know what to write: **What is one change you want to make to your daily routine, and how would you go about doing it?**

Today I have:
Feel free to add your own examples
[ ] exercised for 10 mins
[ ] taken time to relax
[ ] eaten well
[ ] used my support network
[ ] made my bed
[ ] taken my medication
[ ] connected with a friend
[ ] disconnected from technology
[ ]
[ ]
[ ]

Tonight I am anxious about:
* Do not feel obliged to fill in anything here. The purpose is to put on paper anything that is troubling you as you attempt to sleep, doing so can often move the mind away from that thought.

Morning

Aim to complete the left hand page first thing in the morning, BEFORE you first check your phone or similar devices. Doing so helps to give you a solid base prior to the inevitable distractions of e-mail, social media, messages, news etc.

Approx how many hours did I sleep for?	How well rested am I? 1 = exhausted 6 = full of energy	Current Mood 1 = awful 6 = amazing

My priorities today are...

1.

2.

3.

*Reminder: No more than 3, keep them realistic and do not berate yourself if you don't always achieve all 3.

Today I am grateful for...

1.

2.

3.

*Reminder: These can be tiny, but try to not simply repeat the previous day's list

www.iam1in4.com   Find us on Facebook, Twitter & Instagram

Evening

The right hand page can be completed at a time in the day that suits you best.
However, it is recommended to make it part of your evening / bed time routine. By doing so you are able to put some of your concerns aside to help with a better night's sleep.

Journal Entry
* Prompt for if you are struggling to know what to write: Describe a time you sabotaged a situation for yourself and how would you handle it differently in the future

Today I have:
Feel free to add your own examples
[ ] exercised for 10 mins
[ ] taken time to relax
[ ] eaten well
[ ] used my support network
[ ] made my bed
[ ] taken my medication
[ ] connected with a friend
[ ] disconnected from technology
[ ]
[ ]
[ ]

Tonight I am anxious about:
* Do not feel obliged to fill in anything here. The purpose is to put on paper anything that is troubling you as you attempt to sleep, doing so can often move the mind away from that thought.

www.iam1in4.com   Reducing the stigma around mental health

Morning

Aim to complete the left hand page first thing in the morning, BEFORE you first check your phone or similar devices. Doing so helps to give you a solid base prior to the inevitable distractions of e-mail, social media, messages, news etc.

Approx how many hours did I sleep for?	How well rested am I? 1 = exhausted 6 = full of energy	Current Mood 1 = awful 6 = amazing

My priorities today are...

1.

2.

3.

* Reminder: No more than 3, keep them realistic and do not berate yourself if you don't always achieve all 3.

Today I am grateful for...

1.

2.

3.

* Reminder: These can be tiny, but try to not simply repeat the previous day's list

www.iam1in4.com   Find us on Facebook, Twitter & Instagram

Evening

The right hand page can be completed at a time in the day that suits you best.
However, it is recommended to make it part of your evening / bed time routine. By doing so you are able to put some of your concerns aside to help with a better night's sleep.

Journal Entry
* Prompt for if you are struggling to know what to write: **Describe your perfect evening**

Today I have:
Feel free to add your own examples
[ ] exercised for 10 mins
[ ] taken time to relax
[ ] eaten well
[ ] used my support network
[ ] made my bed
[ ] taken my medication
[ ] connected with a friend
[ ] disconnected from technology
[ ]
[ ]
[ ]

Tonight I am anxious about:
* Do not feel obliged to fill in anything here. The purpose is to put on paper anything that is troubling you as you attempt to sleep, doing so can often move the mind away from that thought.

Morning

Aim to complete the left hand page first thing in the morning, BEFORE you first check your phone or similar devices. Doing so helps to give you a solid base prior to the inevitable distractions of e-mail, social media, messages, news etc.

Approx how many hours did I sleep for?	How well rested am I? 1 = exhausted 6 = full of energy	Current Mood 1 = awful 6 = amazing

My priorities today are...

1.

2.

3.

* Reminder: No more than 3, keep them realistic and do not berate yourself if you don't always achieve all 3.

Today I am grateful for...

1.

2.

3.

* Reminder: These can be tiny, but try to not simply repeat the previous day's list

www.iam1in4.com   Find us on Facebook, Twitter & Instagram

Evening

The right hand page can be completed at a time in the day that suits you best.
However, it is recommended to make it part of your evening / bed time routine. By doing so you are able to put some of your concerns aside to help with a better night's sleep.

Journal Entry
* Prompt for if you are struggling to know what to write: What personality traits do you like and admire the most?

Today I have:
Feel free to add your own examples
[ ] exercised for 10 mins
[ ] taken time to relax
[ ] eaten well
[ ] used my support network
[ ] made my bed
[ ] taken my medication
[ ] connected with a friend
[ ] disconnected from technology
[ ]
[ ]
[ ]

Tonight I am anxious about:
* Do not feel obliged to fill in anything here. The purpose is to put on paper anything that is troubling you as you attempt to sleep, doing so can often move the mind away from that thought

www.iam1in4.com   Reducing the stigma around mental health

Morning

Aim to complete the left hand page first thing in the morning, BEFORE you first check your phone or similar devices. Doing so helps to give you a solid base prior to the inevitable distractions of e-mail, social media, messages, news etc.

Approx how many hours did I sleep for?	How well rested am I? 1 = exhausted 6 = full of energy	Current Mood 1 = awful 6 = amazing

My priorities today are...

1.

2.

3.

* Reminder: No more than 3, keep them realistic and do not berate yourself if you don't always achieve all 3.

Today I am grateful for...

1.

2.

3.

* Reminder: These can be tiny, but try to not simply repeat the previous day's list

www.iam1in4.com　　　　　　　　　　Find us on Facebook, Twitter & Instagram

Evening

The right hand page can be completed at a time in the day that suits you best.
However, it is recommended to make it part of your evening / bed time routine. By doing so you are able to put some of your concerns aside to help with a better night's sleep.

Journal Entry
* Prompt for if you are struggling to know what to write: What personality traits do you dislike the most?

Today I have:
Feel free to add your own examples
- [ ] exercised for 10 mins
- [ ] taken time to relax
- [ ] eaten well
- [ ] used my support network
- [ ] made my bed
- [ ] taken my medication
- [ ] connected with a friend
- [ ] disconnected from technology
- [ ]
- [ ]
- [ ]

Tonight I am anxious about:
* Do not feel obliged to fill in anything here. The purpose is to put on paper anything that is troubling you as you attempt to sleep, doing so can often move the mind away from that thought.

Morning

Aim to complete the left hand page first thing in the morning, BEFORE you first check your phone or similar devices. Doing so helps to give you a solid base prior to the inevitable distractions of e-mail, social media, messages, news etc.

Approx how many hours did I sleep for?	How well rested am I? 1 = exhausted 6 = full of energy	Current Mood 1 = awful 6 = amazing

My priorities today are...

1.

2.

3.

* Reminder: No more than 3, keep them realistic and do not berate yourself if you don't always achieve all 3.

Today I am grateful for...

1.

2.

3.

* Reminder: These can be tiny, but try to not simply repeat the previous day's list

www.iam1in4.com   Find us on Facebook, Twitter & Instagram

Evening

The right hand page can be completed at a time in the day that suits you best.
However, it is recommended to make it part of your evening / bed time routine. By doing so you are able to put some of your concerns aside to help with a better night's sleep.

Journal Entry
* Prompt for if you are struggling to know what to write: **What was the last thing that made you laugh out loud?**

Today I have:
Feel free to add your own examples
[ ] exercised for 10 mins
[ ] taken time to relax
[ ] eaten well
[ ] used my support network
[ ] made my bed
[ ] taken my medication
[ ] connected with a friend
[ ] disconnected from technology
[ ]
[ ]
[ ]

Tonight I am anxious about:
* Do not feel obliged to fill in anything here. The purpose is to put on paper anything that is troubling you as you attempt to sleep, doing so can often move the mind away from that thought.

Morning

Aim to complete the left hand page first thing in the morning, BEFORE you first check your phone or similar devices. Doing so helps to give you a solid base prior to the inevitable distractions of e-mail, social media, messages, news etc.

Approx how many hours did I sleep for?	How well rested am I? 1 = exhausted 6 = full of energy	Current Mood 1 = awful 6 = amazing

My priorities today are...

1.

2.

3.

* Reminder: No more than 3, keep them realistic and do not berate yourself if you don't always achieve all 3.

Today I am grateful for...

1.

2.

3.

* Reminder: These can be tiny, but try to not simply repeat the previous day's list

www.iam1in4.com   Find us on Facebook, Twitter & Instagram

Evening

The right hand page can be completed at a time in the day that suits you best.
However, it is recommended to make it part of your evening / bed time routine. By doing so you are able to put some of your concerns aside to help with a better night's sleep.

Journal Entry
* Prompt for if you are struggling to know what to write: **When was the last time you cried?**

Today I have:
Feel free to add your own examples
- [ ] exercised for 10 mins
- [ ] taken time to relax
- [ ] eaten well
- [ ] used my support network
- [ ] made my bed
- [ ] taken my medication
- [ ] connected with a friend
- [ ] disconnected from technology
- [ ]
- [ ]
- [ ]

Tonight I am anxious about:
* Do not feel obliged to fill in anything here. The purpose is to put on paper anything that is troubling you as you attempt to sleep, doing so can often move the mind away from that thought.

www.iam1in4.com   Reducing the stigma around mental health

Morning

Aim to complete the left hand page first thing in the morning, BEFORE you first check your phone or similar devices. Doing so helps to give you a solid base prior to the inevitable distractions of e-mail, social media, messages, news etc.

Approx how many hours did I sleep for?	How well rested am I? 1 = exhausted 6 = full of energy	Current Mood 1 = awful 6 = amazing

My priorities today are...

1.

2.

3.

* Reminder: No more than 3, keep them realistic and do not berate yourself if you don't always achieve all 3.

Today I am grateful for...

1.

2.

3.

* Reminder: These can be tiny, but try to not simply repeat the previous day's list

www.iam1in4.com   Find us on Facebook, Twitter & Instagram

Evening

The right hand page can be completed at a time in the day that suits you best.
However, it is recommended to make it part of your evening / bed time routine. By doing so you are able to put some of your concerns aside to help with a better night's sleep.

Journal Entry
* Prompt for if you are struggling to know what to write: **What are some of your favourite things?**

Today I have:
Feel free to add your own examples
- [ ] exercised for 10 mins
- [ ] taken time to relax
- [ ] eaten well
- [ ] used my support network
- [ ] made my bed
- [ ] taken my medication
- [ ] connected with a friend
- [ ] disconnected from technology
- [ ]
- [ ]
- [ ]

Tonight I am anxious about:
* Do not feel obliged to fill in anything here. The purpose is to put on paper anything that is troubling you as you attempt to sleep, doing so can often move the mind away from that thought.

www.iam1in4.com

Reducing the stigma around mental health

Morning

Aim to complete the left hand page first thing in the morning, BEFORE you first check your phone or similar devices. Doing so helps to give you a solid base prior to the inevitable distractions of e-mail, social media, messages, news etc.

Approx how many hours did I sleep for?	How well rested am I? 1 = exhausted 6 = full of energy	Current Mood 1 = awful 6 = amazing

My priorities today are...

1.

2.

3.

* Reminder: No more than 3, keep them realistic and do not berate yourself if you don't always achieve all 3.

Today I am grateful for...

1.

2.

3.

* Reminder: These can be tiny, but try to not simply repeat the previous day's list

www.iam1in4.com   Find us on Facebook, Twitter & Instagram

Evening

The right hand page can be completed at a time in the day that suits you best.
However, it is recommended to make it part of your evening / bed time routine. By doing so you are able to put some of your concerns aside to help with a better night's sleep.

Journal Entry
* Prompt for if you are struggling to know what to write: **What would your ideal career be?**

Today I have:
Feel free to add your own examples
- [ ] exercised for 10 mins
- [ ] taken time to relax
- [ ] eaten well
- [ ] used my support network
- [ ] made my bed
- [ ] taken my medication
- [ ] connected with a friend
- [ ] disconnected from technology
- [ ]
- [ ]
- [ ]

Tonight I am anxious about:
* Do not feel obliged to fill in anything here. The purpose is to put on paper anything that is troubling you as you attempt to sleep, doing so can often move the mind away from that thought.

www.iam1in4.com — Reducing the stigma around mental health

Morning

Aim to complete the left hand page first thing in the morning, BEFORE you first check your phone or similar devices. Doing so helps to give you a solid base prior to the inevitable distractions of e-mail, social media, messages, news etc.

Approx how many hours did I sleep for?	How well rested am I? 1 = exhausted 6 = full of energy	Current Mood 1 = awful 6 = amazing

My priorities today are...

1.

2.

3.

* Reminder: No more than 3, keep them realistic and do not berate yourself if you don't always achieve all 3.

Today I am grateful for...

1.

2.

3.

* Reminder: These can be tiny, but try to not simply repeat the previous day's list.

www.iam1in4.com   Find us on Facebook, Twitter & Instagram

Evening

The right hand page can be completed at a time in the day that suits you best.
However, it is recommended to make it part of your evening / bed time routine. By doing so you are able to put some of your concerns aside to help with a better night's sleep.

Journal Entry
* Prompt for if you are struggling to know what to write: **What is your biggest achievement?**

Today I have:
Feel free to add your own examples
[ ] exercised for 10 mins
[ ] taken time to relax
[ ] eaten well
[ ] used my support network
[ ] made my bed
[ ] taken my medication
[ ] connected with a friend
[ ] disconnected from technology
[ ]
[ ]
[ ]

Tonight I am anxious about:
* Do not feel obliged to fill in anything here. The purpose is to put on paper anything that is troubling you as you attempt to sleep, doing so can often move the mind away from that thought.

www.iam1in4.com   Reducing the stigma around mental health

Morning

Aim to complete the left hand page first thing in the morning, BEFORE you first check your phone or similar devices. Doing so helps to give you a solid base prior to the inevitable distractions of e-mail, social media, messages, news etc.

Approx how many hours did I sleep for?	How well rested am I? 1 = exhausted 6 = full of energy	Current Mood 1 = awful 6 = amazing

My priorities today are...

1.

2.

3.

* Reminder: No more than 3, keep them realistic and do not berate yourself if you don't always achieve all 3.

Today I am grateful for...

1.

2.

3.

* Reminder: These can be tiny, but try to not simply repeat the previous day's list

www.iam1in4.com   Find us on Facebook, Twitter & Instagram

Evening

The right hand page can be completed at a time in the day that suits you best.
However, it is recommended to make it part of your evening / bed time routine. By doing so you are able to put some of your concerns aside to help with a better night's sleep.

Journal Entry
* Prompt for if you are struggling to know what to write: **What benefits do you notice when you exercise?**

Today I have:
Feel free to add your own examples
[ ] exercised for 10 mins
[ ] taken time to relax
[ ] eaten well
[ ] used my support network
[ ] made my bed
[ ] taken my medication
[ ] connected with a friend
[ ] disconnected from technology
[ ]
[ ]
[ ]

Tonight I am anxious about:
* Do not feel obliged to fill in anything here. The purpose is to put on paper anything that is troubling you as you attempt to sleep, doing so can often move the mind away from that thought.

www.iam1in4.com   Reducing the stigma around mental health

Morning

Aim to complete the left hand page first thing in the morning, BEFORE you first check your phone or similar devices. Doing so helps to give you a solid base prior to the inevitable distractions of e-mail, social media, messages, news etc.

Approx how many hours did I sleep for?	How well rested am I? 1 = exhausted 6 = full of energy	Current Mood 1 = awful 6 = amazing

My priorities today are...

1.

2.

3.

* Reminder: No more than 3, keep them realistic and do not berate yourself if you don't always achieve all 3.

Today I am grateful for...

1.

2.

3.

* Reminder: These can be tiny, but try to not simply repeat the previous day's list

www.iam1in4.com Find us on Facebook, Twitter & Instagram

Evening

The right hand page can be completed at a time in the day that suits you best.
However, it is recommended to make it part of your evening / bed time routine. By doing so you are able to put some of your concerns aside to help with a better night's sleep.

Journal Entry
* Prompt for if you are struggling to know what to write: **What helps to calm you when anxiety begins to build?**

Today I have:
Feel free to add your own examples
- [ ] exercised for 10 mins
- [ ] taken time to relax
- [ ] eaten well
- [ ] used my support network
- [ ] made my bed
- [ ] taken my medication
- [ ] connected with a friend
- [ ] disconnected from technology
- [ ]
- [ ]
- [ ]

Tonight I am anxious about:
* Do not feel obliged to fill in anything here. The purpose is to put on paper anything that is troubling you as you attempt to sleep, doing so can often move the mind away from that thought.

www.iam1in4.com   Reducing the stigma around mental health

Morning

Aim to complete the left hand page first thing in the morning, BEFORE you first check your phone or similar devices. Doing so helps to give you a solid base prior to the inevitable distractions of e-mail, social media, messages, news etc.

Approx how many hours did I sleep for?	How well rested am I? 1 = exhausted 6 = full of energy	Current Mood 1 = awful 6 = amazing

My priorities today are...

1.

2.

3.

* Reminder: No more than 3, keep them realistic and do not berate yourself if you don't always achieve all 3.

Today I am grateful for...

1.

2.

3.

* Reminder: These can be tiny, but try to not simply repeat the previous day's list

www.iam1in4.com   Find us on Facebook, Twitter & Instagram

Evening

The right hand page can be completed at a time in the day that suits you best.
However, it is recommended to make it part of your evening / bed time routine. By doing so you are able to put some of your concerns aside to help with a better night's sleep.

Journal Entry
* Prompt for if you are struggling to know what to write: **What about today do you wish you could do again tomorrow?**

Today I have:
Feel free to add your own examples
- [ ] exercised for 10 mins
- [ ] taken time to relax
- [ ] eaten well
- [ ] used my support network
- [ ] made my bed
- [ ] taken my medication
- [ ] connected with a friend
- [ ] disconnected from technology
- [ ]
- [ ]
- [ ]

Tonight I am anxious about:
* Do not feel obliged to fill in anything here. The purpose is to put on paper anything that is troubling you as you attempt to sleep, doing so can often move the mind away from that thought.

www.iam1in4.com

Reducing the stigma around mental health

Morning

Aim to complete the left hand page first thing in the morning, BEFORE you first check your phone or similar devices. Doing so helps to give you a solid base prior to the inevitable distractions of e-mail, social media, messages, news etc.

Approx how many hours did I sleep for?	How well rested am I? 1 = exhausted 6 = full of energy	Current Mood 1 = awful 6 = amazing

My priorities today are...

1.

2.

3.

* Reminder: No more than 3, keep them realistic and do not berate yourself if you don't always achieve all 3.

Today I am grateful for...

1.

2.

3.

* Reminder: These can be tiny, but try to not simply repeat the previous day's list

www.iam1in4.com   Find us on Facebook, Twitter & Instagram

Evening

The right hand page can be completed at a time in the day that suits you best.
However, it is recommended to make it part of your evening / bed time routine. By doing so you are able to put some of your concerns aside to help with a better night's sleep.

Journal Entry
* Prompt for if you are struggling to know what to write: Write about a song from your childhood that always puts a smile on your face

Today I have:
Feel free to add your own examples

[ ] exercised for 10 mins
[ ] taken time to relax
[ ] eaten well
[ ] used my support network
[ ] made my bed
[ ] taken my medication
[ ] connected with a friend
[ ] disconnected from technology
[ ]
[ ]
[ ]

Tonight I am anxious about:
* Do not feel obliged to fill in anything here. The purpose is to put on paper anything that is troubling you as you attempt to sleep, doing so can often move the mind away from that thought.

www.iam1in4.com

Reducing the stigma around mental health

Morning

Aim to complete the left hand page first thing in the morning, BEFORE you first check your phone or similar devices. Doing so helps to give you a solid base prior to the inevitable distractions of e-mail, social media, messages, news etc.

Approx how many hours did I sleep for?	How well rested am I? 1 = exhausted 6 = full of energy	Current Mood 1 = awful 6 = amazing

My priorities today are...

1.

2.

3.

* Reminder: No more than 3, keep them realistic and do not berate yourself if you don't always achieve all 3.

Today I am grateful for...

1.

2.

3.

* Reminder: These can be tiny, but try to not simply repeat the previous day's list

www.iam1in4.com   Find us on Facebook, Twitter & Instagram

Evening

The right hand page can be completed at a time in the day that suits you best.
However, it is recommended to make it part of your evening / bed time routine. By doing so you are able to put some of your concerns aside to help with a better night's sleep.

Journal Entry
* Prompt for if you are struggling to know what to write: **Describe one of your earliest memories**

Today I have:
Feel free to add your own examples
[ ] exercised for 10 mins
[ ] taken time to relax
[ ] eaten well
[ ] used my support network
[ ] made my bed
[ ] taken my medication
[ ] connected with a friend
[ ] disconnected from technology
[ ]
[ ]
[ ]

Tonight I am anxious about:
* Do not feel obliged to fill in anything here. The purpose is to put on paper anything that is troubling you as you attempt to sleep, doing so can often move the mind away from that thought.

www.iam1in4.com — Reducing the stigma around mental health

Morning

Aim to complete the left hand page first thing in the morning, BEFORE you first check your phone or similar devices. Doing so helps to give you a solid base prior to the inevitable distractions of e-mail, social media, messages, news etc.

Approx how many hours did I sleep for?	How well rested am I? 1 = exhausted 6 = full of energy	Current Mood 1 = awful 6 = amazing

My priorities today are...

1.

2.

3.

* Reminder: No more than 3, keep them realistic and do not berate yourself if you don't always achieve all 3.

Today I am grateful for...

1.

2.

3.

* Reminder: These can be tiny, but try to not simply repeat the previous day's list

www.iam1in4.com   Find us on Facebook, Twitter & Instagram

Evening

The right hand page can be completed at a time in the day that suits you best.
However, it is recommended to make it part of your evening / bed time routine. By doing so you are able to put some of your concerns aside to help with a better night's sleep.

Journal Entry
* Prompt for if you are struggling to know what to write: **What are your top long term goals?**

Today I have:
Feel free to add your own examples

[ ] exercised for 10 mins
[ ] taken time to relax
[ ] eaten well
[ ] used my support network
[ ] made my bed
[ ] taken my medication
[ ] connected with a friend
[ ] disconnected from technology
[ ]
[ ]
[ ]

Tonight I am anxious about:
* Do not feel obliged to fill in anything here. The purpose is to put on paper anything that is troubling you as you attempt to sleep, doing so can often move the mind away from that thought.

Morning

Aim to complete the left hand page first thing in the morning, BEFORE you first check your phone or similar devices. Doing so helps to give you a solid base prior to the inevitable distractions of e-mail, social media, messages, news etc.

Approx how many hours did I sleep for?	How well rested am I? 1 = exhausted 6 = full of energy	Current Mood 1 = awful 6 = amazing

My priorities today are...

1.

2.

3.

* Reminder: No more than 3, keep them realistic and do not berate yourself if you don't always achieve all 3.

Today I am grateful for...

1.

2.

3.

* Reminder: These can be tiny, but try to not simply repeat the previous day's list

www.iam1in4.com   Find us on Facebook, Twitter & Instagram

Evening

The right hand page can be completed at a time in the day that suits you best.
However, it is recommended to make it part of your evening / bed time routine. By doing so you are able to put some of your concerns aside to help with a better night's sleep.

Journal Entry
* Prompt for if you are struggling to know what to write: **What does nobody know about you?**

Today I have:
Feel free to add your own examples

[ ] exercised for 10 mins
[ ] taken time to relax
[ ] eaten well
[ ] used my support network
[ ] made my bed
[ ] taken my medication
[ ] connected with a friend
[ ] disconnected from technology
[ ]
[ ]
[ ]

Tonight I am anxious about:
* Do not feel obliged to fill in anything here. The purpose is to put on paper anything that is troubling you as you attempt to sleep, doing so can often move the mind away from that thought.

www.iam1in4.com Reducing the stigma around mental health

Morning

Aim to complete the left hand page first thing in the morning, BEFORE you first check your phone or similar devices. Doing so helps to give you a solid base prior to the inevitable distractions of e-mail, social media, messages, news etc.

Approx how many hours did I sleep for?	How well rested am I? 1 = exhausted 6 = full of energy	Current Mood 1 = awful 6 = amazing

My priorities today are...

1.

2.

3.

* Reminder: No more than 3, keep them realistic and do not berate yourself if you don't always achieve all 3.

Today I am grateful for...

1.

2.

3.

* Reminder: These can be tiny, but try to not simply repeat the previous day's list

www.iam1in4.com   Find us on Facebook, Twitter & Instagram

Evening

The right hand page can be completed at a time in the day that suits you best.
However, it is recommended to make it part of your evening / bed time routine. By doing so you are able to put some of your concerns aside to help with a better night's sleep.

Journal Entry
* Prompt for if you are struggling to know what to write: **What was the most fun you ever had?**

Today I have:
Feel free to add your own examples

[ ] exercised for 10 mins
[ ] taken time to relax
[ ] eaten well
[ ] used my support network
[ ] made my bed
[ ] taken my medication
[ ] connected with a friend
[ ] disconnected from technology
[ ]
[ ]
[ ]

Tonight I am anxious about:
* Do not feel obliged to fill in anything here. The purpose is to put on paper anything that is troubling you as you attempt to sleep, doing so can often move the mind away from that thought.

www.iam1in4.com   Reducing the stigma around mental health

Morning

Aim to complete the left hand page first thing in the morning, BEFORE you first check your phone or similar devices. Doing so helps to give you a solid base prior to the inevitable distractions of e-mail, social media, messages, news etc.

Approx how many hours did I sleep for?	How well rested am I? 1 = exhausted 6 = full of energy	Current Mood 1 = awful 6 = amazing

My priorities today are...

1.

2.

3.

* Reminder: No more than 3, keep them realistic and do not berate yourself if you don't always achieve all 3.

Today I am grateful for...

1.

2.

3.

* Reminder: These can be tiny, but try to not simply repeat the previous day's list

www.iam1in4.com   Find us on Facebook, Twitter & Instagram

Evening

The right hand page can be completed at a time in the day that suits you best.
However, it is recommended to make it part of your evening / bed time routine. By doing so you are able to put some of your concerns aside to help with a better night's sleep.

Journal Entry
* Prompt for if you are struggling to know what to write: **What are 3 things you can't do without?**

Today I have:
Feel free to add your own examples

- [ ] exercised for 10 mins
- [ ] taken time to relax
- [ ] eaten well
- [ ] used my support network
- [ ] made my bed
- [ ] taken my medication
- [ ] connected with a friend
- [ ] disconnected from technology
- [ ]
- [ ]
- [ ]

Tonight I am anxious about:
* Do not feel obliged to fill in anything here. The purpose is to put on paper anything that is troubling you as you attempt to sleep, doing so can often move the mind away from that thought.

www.iam1in4.com   Reducing the stigma around mental health

Morning

Aim to complete the left hand page first thing in the morning, BEFORE you first check your phone or similar devices. Doing so helps to give you a solid base prior to the inevitable distractions of e-mail, social media, messages, news etc.

Approx how many hours did I sleep for?	How well rested am I? 1 = exhausted 6 = full of energy	Current Mood 1 = awful 6 = amazing

My priorities today are...

1.

2.

3.

* Reminder: No more than 3, keep them realistic and do not berate yourself if you don't always achieve all 3.

Today I am grateful for...

1.

2.

3.

* Reminder: These can be tiny, but try to not simply repeat the previous day's list

www.iam1in4.com   Find us on Facebook, Twitter & Instagram

Evening

The right hand page can be completed at a time in the day that suits you best. However, it is recommended to make it part of your evening / bed time routine. By doing so you are able to put some of your concerns aside to help with a better night's sleep.

Journal Entry
* Prompt for if you are struggling to know what to write: **What are your pet peeves?**

Today I have:
Feel free to add your own examples
[ ] exercised for 10 mins
[ ] taken time to relax
[ ] eaten well
[ ] used my support network
[ ] made my bed
[ ] taken my medication
[ ] connected with a friend
[ ] disconnected from technology
[ ]
[ ]
[ ]

Tonight I am anxious about:
* Do not feel obliged to fill in anything here. The purpose is to put on paper anything that is troubling you as you attempt to sleep, doing so can often move the mind away from that thought.

www.iam1in4.com Reducing the stigma around mental health

Morning

Aim to complete the left hand page first thing in the morning, BEFORE you first check your phone or similar devices. Doing so helps to give you a solid base prior to the inevitable distractions of e-mail, social media, messages, news etc.

Approx how many hours did I sleep for?	How well rested am I? 1 = exhausted 6 = full of energy	Current Mood 1 = awful 6 = amazing

My priorities today are...

1.

2.

3.

* Reminder: No more than 3, keep them realistic and do not berate yourself if you don't always achieve all 3.

Today I am grateful for...

1.

2.

3.

* Reminder: These can be tiny, but try to not simply repeat the previous day's list

www.iam1in4.com   Find us on Facebook, Twitter & Instagram

Evening

The right hand page can be completed at a time in the day that suits you best.
However, it is recommended to make it part of your evening / bed time routine. By doing so you are able to put some of your concerns aside to help with a better night's sleep.

Journal Entry
* Prompt for if you are struggling to know what to write: What quote really means a lot to you?

Today I have:
Feel free to add your own examples
[ ] exercised for 10 mins
[ ] taken time to relax
[ ] eaten well
[ ] used my support network
[ ] made my bed
[ ] taken my medication
[ ] connected with a friend
[ ] disconnected from technology
[ ]
[ ]
[ ]

Tonight I am anxious about:
* Do not feel obliged to fill in anything here. The purpose is to put on paper anything that is troubling you as you attempt to sleep, doing so can often move the mind away from that thought.

www.iam1in4.com   Reducing the stigma around mental health

Morning

Aim to complete the left hand page first thing in the morning, BEFORE you first check your phone or similar devices. Doing so helps to give you a solid base prior to the inevitable distractions of e-mail, social media, messages, news etc.

Approx how many hours did I sleep for?	How well rested am I? 1 = exhausted 6 = full of energy	Current Mood 1 = awful 6 = amazing

My priorities today are...

1.

2.

3.

* Reminder: No more than 3, keep them realistic and do not berate yourself if you don't always achieve all 3.

Today I am grateful for...

1.

2.

3.

* Reminder: These can be tiny, but try to not simply repeat the previous day's list

www.iam1in4.com   Find us on Facebook, Twitter & Instagram

Evening

The right hand page can be completed at a time in the day that suits you best.
However, it is recommended to make it part of your evening / bed time routine. By doing so you are able to put some of your concerns aside to help with a better night's sleep.

Journal Entry
*Prompt for if you are struggling to know what to write: **How well do you deal with anger?**

Today I have:
Feel free to add your own examples

[ ] exercised for 10 mins
[ ] taken time to relax
[ ] eaten well
[ ] used my support network
[ ] made my bed
[ ] taken my medication
[ ] connected with a friend
[ ] disconnected from technology
[ ]
[ ]
[ ]

Tonight I am anxious about:
* Do not feel obliged to fill in anything here. The purpose is to put on paper anything that is troubling you as you attempt to sleep, doing so can often move the mind away from that thought.

www.iam1in4.com   Reducing the stigma around mental health

Morning

Aim to complete the left hand page first thing in the morning, BEFORE you first check your phone or similar devices. Doing so helps to give you a solid base prior to the inevitable distractions of e-mail, social media, messages, news etc.

Approx how many hours did I sleep for?	How well rested am I? 1 = exhausted 6 = full of energy	Current Mood 1 = awful 6 = amazing

My priorities today are...

1.

2.

3.

* Reminder: No more than 3, keep them realistic and do not berate yourself if you don't always achieve all 3.

Today I am grateful for...

1.

2.

3.

* Reminder: These can be tiny, but try to not simply repeat the previous day's list

www.iam1in4.com   Find us on Facebook, Twitter & Instagram

Evening

The right hand page can be completed at a time in the day that suits you best.
However, it is recommended to make it part of your evening / bed time routine. By doing so you are able to put some of your concerns aside to help with a better night's sleep.

Journal Entry
* Prompt for if you are struggling to know what to write: **What is the main emotion in your life right now?**

Today I have:
Feel free to add your own examples
[ ] exercised for 10 mins
[ ] taken time to relax
[ ] eaten well
[ ] used my support network
[ ] made my bed
[ ] taken my medication
[ ] connected with a friend
[ ] disconnected from technology
[ ]
[ ]
[ ]

Tonight I am anxious about:
* Do not feel obliged to fill in anything here. The purpose is to put on paper anything that is troubling you as you attempt to sleep, doing so can often move the mind away from that thought.

www.iam1in4.com   Reducing the stigma around mental health

Morning

Aim to complete the left hand page first thing in the morning, BEFORE you first check your phone or similar devices. Doing so helps to give you a solid base prior to the inevitable distractions of e-mail, social media, messages, news etc.

Approx how many hours did I sleep for?	How well rested am I? 1 = exhausted 6 = full of energy	Current Mood 1 = awful 6 = amazing

My priorities today are...

1.

2.

3.

* Reminder: No more than 3, keep them realistic and do not berate yourself if you don't always achieve all 3.

Today I am grateful for...

1.

2.

3.

* Reminder: These can be tiny, but try to not simply repeat the previous day's list

www.iam1in4.com   Find us on Facebook, Twitter & Instagram

Evening

The right hand page can be completed at a time in the day that suits you best.
However, it is recommended to make it part of your evening / bed time routine. By doing so you are able to put some of your concerns aside to help with a better night's sleep.

Journal Entry
* Prompt for if you are struggling to know what to write: **When was the last time you told someone a secret of yours?**

Today I have:
Feel free to add your own examples
[ ] exercised for 10 mins
[ ] taken time to relax
[ ] eaten well
[ ] used my support network
[ ] made my bed
[ ] taken my medication
[ ] connected with a friend
[ ] disconnected from technology
[ ]
[ ]
[ ]

Tonight I am anxious about:
* Do not feel obliged to fill in anything here. The purpose is to put on paper anything that is troubling you as you attempt to sleep, doing so can often move the mind away from that thought.

Morning

Aim to complete the left hand page first thing in the morning, BEFORE you first check your phone or similar devices. Doing so helps to give you a solid base prior to the inevitable distractions of e-mail, social media, messages, news etc.

Approx how many hours did I sleep for?	How well rested am I? 1 = exhausted 6 = full of energy	Current Mood 1 = awful 6 = amazing

My priorities today are...

1.

2.

3.

* Reminder: No more than 3, keep them realistic and do not berate yourself if you don't always achieve all 3.

Today I am grateful for...

1.

2.

3.

* Reminder: These can be tiny, but try to not simply repeat the previous day's list

www.iam1in4.com   Find us on Facebook, Twitter & Instagram

Evening

The right hand page can be completed at a time in the day that suits you best.
However, it is recommended to make it part of your evening / bed time routine. By doing so you are able to put some of your concerns aside to help with a better night's sleep.

Journal Entry
* Prompt for if you are struggling to know what to write: **How easily are you able to forgive someone who causes you pain?**

Today I have:
Feel free to add your own examples
[ ] exercised for 10 mins
[ ] taken time to relax
[ ] eaten well
[ ] used my support network
[ ] made my bed
[ ] taken my medication
[ ] connected with a friend
[ ] disconnected from technology
[ ]
[ ]
[ ]

Tonight I am anxious about:
* Do not feel obliged to fill in anything here. The purpose is to put on paper anything that is troubling you as you attempt to sleep, doing so can often move the mind away from that thought.

Morning

Aim to complete the left hand page first thing in the morning, BEFORE you first check your phone or similar devices. Doing so helps to give you a solid base prior to the inevitable distractions of e-mail, social media, messages, news etc.

Approx how many hours did I sleep for?	How well rested am I? 1 = exhausted 6 = full of energy	Current Mood 1 = awful 6 = amazing

My priorities today are...

1.

2.

3.

*Reminder: No more than 3, keep them realistic and do not berate yourself if you don't always achieve all 3.

Today I am grateful for...

1.

2.

3.

*Reminder: These can be tiny, but try to not simply repeat the previous day's list

www.iam1in4.com   Find us on Facebook, Twitter & Instagram

Evening

The right hand page can be completed at a time in the day that suits you best.
However, it is recommended to make it part of your evening / bed time routine. By doing so you are able to put some of your concerns aside to help with a better night's sleep.

Journal Entry
* Prompt for if you are struggling to know what to write: **Write a letter to someone you want to thank**

Today I have:
Feel free to add your own examples

- [ ] exercised for 10 mins
- [ ] taken time to relax
- [ ] eaten well
- [ ] used my support network
- [ ] made my bed
- [ ] taken my medication
- [ ] connected with a friend
- [ ] disconnected from technology
- [ ]
- [ ]
- [ ]

Tonight I am anxious about:
* Do not feel obliged to fill in anything here. The purpose is to put on paper anything that is troubling you as you attempt to sleep, doing so can often move the mind away from that thought.

www.iam1in4.com   Reducing the stigma around mental health

Morning

Aim to complete the left hand page first thing in the morning, BEFORE you first check your phone or similar devices. Doing so helps to give you a solid base prior to the inevitable distractions of e-mail, social media, messages, news etc.

Approx how many hours did I sleep for?	How well rested am I? 1 = exhausted 6 = full of energy	Current Mood 1 = awful 6 = amazing

My priorities today are...

1.

2.

3.

*Reminder: No more than 3, keep them realistic and do not berate yourself if you don't always achieve all 3.

Today I am grateful for...

1.

2.

3.

*Reminder: These can be tiny, but try to not simply repeat the previous day's list

www.iam1in4.com   Find us on Facebook, Twitter & Instagram

Evening

The right hand page can be completed at a time in the day that suits you best. However, it is recommended to make it part of your evening / bed time routine. By doing so you are able to put some of your concerns aside to help with a better night's sleep.

Journal Entry
* Prompt for if you are struggling to know what to write: **How did you feel on your first day at school or in a new job?**

Today I have:
Feel free to add your own examples

[ ] exercised for 10 mins
[ ] taken time to relax
[ ] eaten well
[ ] used my support network
[ ] made my bed
[ ] taken my medication
[ ] connected with a friend
[ ] disconnected from technology
[ ]
[ ]
[ ]

Tonight I am anxious about:
* Do not feel obliged to fill in anything here. The purpose is to put on paper anything that is troubling you as you attempt to sleep, doing so can often move the mind away from that thought.

www.iam1in4.com — Reducing the stigma around mental health

Morning

Aim to complete the left hand page first thing in the morning, BEFORE you first check your phone or similar devices. Doing so helps to give you a solid base prior to the inevitable distractions of e-mail, social media, messages, news etc.

Approx how many hours did I sleep for?	How well rested am I? 1 = exhausted 6 = full of energy	Current Mood 1 = awful 6 = amazing

My priorities today are...

1.

2.

3.

* Reminder: No more than 3, keep them realistic and do not berate yourself if you don't always achieve all 3.

Today I am grateful for...

1.

2.

3.

* Reminder: These can be tiny, but try to not simply repeat the previous day's list

www.iam1in4.com   Find us on Facebook, Twitter & Instagram

Evening

The right hand page can be completed at a time in the day that suits you best. However, it is recommended to make it part of your evening / bed time routine. By doing so you are able to put some of your concerns aside to help with a better night's sleep.

Journal Entry
* Prompt for if you are struggling to know what to write: **What would you do if money didn't matter?**

Today I have:
Feel free to add your own examples
- [ ] exercised for 10 mins
- [ ] taken time to relax
- [ ] eaten well
- [ ] used my support network
- [ ] made my bed
- [ ] taken my medication
- [ ] connected with a friend
- [ ] disconnected from technology
- [ ]
- [ ]
- [ ]

Tonight I am anxious about:
* Do not feel obliged to fill in anything here. The purpose is to put on paper anything that is troubling you as you attempt to sleep, doing so can often move the mind away from that thought.

www.iam1in4.com — Reducing the stigma around mental health

Morning

Aim to complete the left hand page first thing in the morning, BEFORE you first check your phone or similar devices. Doing so helps to give you a solid base prior to the inevitable distractions of e-mail, social media, messages, news etc.

Approx how many hours did I sleep for?	How well rested am I? 1 = exhausted 6 = full of energy	Current Mood 1 = awful 6 = amazing

My priorities today are...

1.

2.

3.

* Reminder: No more than 3, keep them realistic and do not berate yourself if you don't always achieve all 3.

Today I am grateful for...

1.

2.

3.

* Reminder: These can be tiny, but try to not simply repeat the previous day's list

www.iam1in4.com   Find us on Facebook, Twitter & Instagram

Evening

The right hand page can be completed at a time in the day that suits you best.
However, it is recommended to make it part of your evening / bed time routine. By doing so you are able to put some of your concerns aside to help with a better night's sleep.

Journal Entry
* Prompt for if you are struggling to know what to write: **What makes you unique?**

Today I have:
Feel free to add your own examples
- [ ] exercised for 10 mins
- [ ] taken time to relax
- [ ] eaten well
- [ ] used my support network
- [ ] made my bed
- [ ] taken my medication
- [ ] connected with a friend
- [ ] disconnected from technology
- [ ]
- [ ]
- [ ]

Tonight I am anxious about:
* Do not feel obliged to fill in anything here. The purpose is to put on paper anything that is troubling you as you attempt to sleep, doing so can often move the mind away from that thought.

Morning

Aim to complete the left hand page first thing in the morning, BEFORE you first check your phone or similar devices. Doing so helps to give you a solid base prior to the inevitable distractions of e-mail, social media, messages, news etc.

Approx how many hours did I sleep for?	How well rested am I? 1 = exhausted 6 = full of energy	Current Mood 1 = awful 6 = amazing

My priorities today are...

1.

2.

3.

* Reminder: No more than 3, keep them realistic and do not berate yourself if you don't always achieve all 3.

Today I am grateful for...

1.

2.

3.

* Reminder: These can be tiny, but try to not simply repeat the previous day's list

www.iam1in4.com   Find us on Facebook, Twitter & Instagram

Evening

The right hand page can be completed at a time in the day that suits you best.
However, it is recommended to make it part of your evening / bed time routine. By doing so you are able to put some of your concerns aside to help with a better night's sleep.

Journal Entry
* Prompt for if you are struggling to know what to write: **What are you really good at?**

Today I have:
Feel free to add your own examples
[ ] exercised for 10 mins
[ ] taken time to relax
[ ] eaten well
[ ] used my support network
[ ] made my bed
[ ] taken my medication
[ ] connected with a friend
[ ] disconnected from technology
[ ]
[ ]
[ ]

Tonight I am anxious about:
* Do not feel obliged to fill in anything here. The purpose is to put on paper anything that is troubling you as you attempt to sleep, doing so can often move the mind away from that thought.

www.iam1in4.com   Reducing the stigma around mental health

Morning

Aim to complete the left hand page first thing in the morning, BEFORE you first check your phone or similar devices. Doing so helps to give you a solid base prior to the inevitable distractions of e-mail, social media, messages, news etc.

Approx how many hours did I sleep for?	How well rested am I? 1 = exhausted 6 = full of energy	Current Mood 1 = awful 6 = amazing

My priorities today are...

1.

2.

3.

* Reminder: No more than 3, keep them realistic and do not berate yourself if you don't always achieve all 3.

Today I am grateful for...

1.

2.

3.

* Reminder: These can be tiny, but try to not simply repeat the previous day's list

www.iam1in4.com   Find us on Facebook, Twitter & Instagram

Evening

The right hand page can be completed at a time in the day that suits you best.
However, it is recommended to make it part of your evening / bed time routine. By doing so you are able to put some of your concerns aside to help with a better night's sleep.

Journal Entry
* Prompt for if you are struggling to know what to write: **What do you do when you need to practice self-care?**

Today I have:
Feel free to add your own examples
[ ] exercised for 10 mins
[ ] taken time to relax
[ ] eaten well
[ ] used my support network
[ ] made my bed
[ ] taken my medication
[ ] connected with a friend
[ ] disconnected from technology
[ ]
[ ]
[ ]

Tonight I am anxious about:
* Do not feel obliged to fill in anything here. The purpose is to put on paper anything that is troubling you as you attempt to sleep, doing so can often move the mind away from that thought.

www.iam1in4.com   Reducing the stigma around mental health

Morning

Aim to complete the left hand page first thing in the morning, BEFORE you first check your phone or similar devices. Doing so helps to give you a solid base prior to the inevitable distractions of e-mail, social media, messages, news etc.

Approx how many hours did I sleep for?	How well rested am I? 1 = exhausted 6 = full of energy	Current Mood 1 = awful 6 = amazing

My priorities today are...

1.

2.

3.

* Reminder: No more than 3, keep them realistic and do not berate yourself if you don't always achieve all 3.

Today I am grateful for...

1.

2.

3.

* Reminder: These can be tiny, but try to not simply repeat the previous day's list

www.iam1in4.com   Find us on Facebook, Twitter & Instagram

Evening

The right hand page can be completed at a time in the day that suits you best.
However, it is recommended to make it part of your evening / bed time routine. By doing so you are able to put some of your concerns aside to help with a better night's sleep.

Journal Entry
* Prompt for if you are struggling to know what to write: **How do you want to improve the world?**

Today I have:
Feel free to add your own examples
- [ ] exercised for 10 mins
- [ ] taken time to relax
- [ ] eaten well
- [ ] used my support network
- [ ] made my bed
- [ ] taken my medication
- [ ] connected with a friend
- [ ] disconnected from technology
- [ ]
- [ ]
- [ ]

Tonight I am anxious about:
* Do not feel obliged to fill in anything here. The purpose is to put on paper anything that is troubling you as you attempt to sleep, doing so can often move the mind away from that thought.

www.iam1in4.com   Reducing the stigma around mental health

Morning

Aim to complete the left hand page first thing in the morning, BEFORE you first check your phone or similar devices. Doing so helps to give you a solid base prior to the inevitable distractions of e-mail, social media, messages, news etc.

Approx how many hours did I sleep for?	How well rested am I? 1 = exhausted 6 = full of energy	Current Mood 1 = awful 6 = amazing

My priorities today are...

1.

2.

3.

* Reminder: No more than 3, keep them realistic and do not berate yourself if you don't always achieve all 3.

Today I am grateful for...

1.

2.

3.

* Reminder: These can be tiny, but try to not simply repeat the previous day's list

www.iam1in4.com   Find us on Facebook, Twitter & Instagram

Evening

The right hand page can be completed at a time in the day that suits you best.
However, it is recommended to make it part of your evening / bed time routine. By doing so you are able to put some of your concerns aside to help with a better night's sleep.

Journal Entry
* Prompt for if you are struggling to know what to write: **What event would you like to attend?**

Today I have:
Feel free to add your own examples
[ ] exercised for 10 mins
[ ] taken time to relax
[ ] eaten well
[ ] used my support network
[ ] made my bed
[ ] taken my medication
[ ] connected with a friend
[ ] disconnected from technology
[ ]
[ ]
[ ]

Tonight I am anxious about:
* Do not feel obliged to fill in anything here. The purpose is to put on paper anything that is troubling you as you attempt to sleep, doing so can often move the mind away from that thought.

www.iam1in4.com   Reducing the stigma around mental health

Morning

Aim to complete the left hand page first thing in the morning, BEFORE you first check your phone or similar devices. Doing so helps to give you a solid base prior to the inevitable distractions of e-mail, social media, messages, news etc.

Approx how many hours did I sleep for?	How well rested am I? 1 = exhausted 6 = full of energy	Current Mood 1 = awful 6 = amazing

My priorities today are...

1.

2.

3.

* Reminder: No more than 3, keep them realistic and do not berate yourself if you don't always achieve all 3.

Today I am grateful for...

1.

2.

3.

* Reminder: These can be tiny, but try to not simply repeat the previous day's list

www.iam1in4.com   Find us on Facebook, Twitter & Instagram

Evening

The right hand page can be completed at a time in the day that suits you best.
However, it is recommended to make it part of your evening / bed time routine. By doing so you are able to put some of your concerns aside to help with a better night's sleep.

Journal Entry
*Prompt for if you are struggling to know what to write: **What song instantly reminds you of a happy time?**

Today I have:
Feel free to add your own examples
- [ ] exercised for 10 mins
- [ ] taken time to relax
- [ ] eaten well
- [ ] used my support network
- [ ] made my bed
- [ ] taken my medication
- [ ] connected with a friend
- [ ] disconnected from technology
- [ ]
- [ ]
- [ ]

Tonight I am anxious about:
*Do not feel obliged to fill in anything here. The purpose is to put on paper anything that is troubling you as you attempt to sleep, doing so can often move the mind away from that thought.

www.iam1in4.com   Reducing the stigma around mental health

Morning

Aim to complete the left hand page first thing in the morning, BEFORE you first check your phone or similar devices. Doing so helps to give you a solid base prior to the inevitable distractions of e-mail, social media, messages, news etc.

Approx how many hours did I sleep for?	How well rested am I? 1 = exhausted 6 = full of energy	Current Mood 1 = awful 6 = amazing

My priorities today are...

1.

2.

3.

* Reminder: No more than 3, keep them realistic and do not berate yourself if you don't always achieve all 3.

Today I am grateful for...

1.

2.

3.

* Reminder: These can be tiny, but try to not simply repeat the previous day's list

www.iam1in4.com   Find us on Facebook, Twitter & Instagram

Evening

The right hand page can be completed at a time in the day that suits you best.
However, it is recommended to make it part of your evening / bed time routine. By doing so you are able to put some of your concerns aside to help with a better night's sleep.

Journal Entry
* Prompt for if you are struggling to know what to write: **What do you look for in a friend?**

Today I have:
Feel free to add your own examples
[ ] exercised for 10 mins
[ ] taken time to relax
[ ] eaten well
[ ] used my support network
[ ] made my bed
[ ] taken my medication
[ ] connected with a friend
[ ] disconnected from technology
[ ]
[ ]
[ ]

Tonight I am anxious about:
* Do not feel obliged to fill in anything here. The purpose is to put on paper anything that is troubling you as you attempt to sleep, doing so can often move the mind away from that thought.

Morning

Aim to complete the left hand page first thing in the morning, BEFORE you first check your phone or similar devices. Doing so helps to give you a solid base prior to the inevitable distractions of e-mail, social media, messages, news etc.

Approx how many hours did I sleep for?	How well rested am I? 1 = exhausted 6 = full of energy	Current Mood 1 = awful 6 = amazing

My priorities today are...

1.

2.

3.

* Reminder: No more than 3, keep them realistic and do not berate yourself if you don't always achieve all 3.

Today I am grateful for...

1.

2.

3.

* Reminder: These can be tiny, but try to not simply repeat the previous day's list

www.iam1in4.com   Find us on Facebook, Twitter & Instagram

Evening

The right hand page can be completed at a time in the day that suits you best.
However, it is recommended to make it part of your evening / bed time routine. By doing so you are able to put some of your concerns aside to help with a better night's sleep.

Journal Entry
* Prompt for if you are struggling to know what to write: **How would you describe yourself?**

Today I have:
Feel free to add your own examples
[ ] exercised for 10 mins
[ ] taken time to relax
[ ] eaten well
[ ] used my support network
[ ] made my bed
[ ] taken my medication
[ ] connected with a friend
[ ] disconnected from technology
[ ]
[ ]
[ ]

Tonight I am anxious about:
* Do not feel obliged to fill in anything here. The purpose is to put on paper anything that is troubling you as you attempt to sleep, doing so can often move the mind away from that thought.

www.iam1in4.com   Reducing the stigma around mental health

Morning

Aim to complete the left hand page first thing in the morning, BEFORE you first check your phone or similar devices. Doing so helps to give you a solid base prior to the inevitable distractions of e-mail, social media, messages, news etc.

Approx how many hours did I sleep for?	How well rested am I? 1 = exhausted 6 = full of energy	Current Mood 1 = awful 6 = amazing

My priorities today are...

1.

2.

3.

* Reminder: No more than 3, keep them realistic and do not berate yourself if you don't always achieve all 3.

Today I am grateful for...

1.

2.

3.

* Reminder: These can be tiny, but try to not simply repeat the previous day's list

www.iam1in4.com   Find us on Facebook, Twitter & Instagram

Evening

The right hand page can be completed at a time in the day that suits you best.
However, it is recommended to make it part of your evening / bed time routine. By doing so you are able to put some of your concerns aside to help with a better night's sleep.

Journal Entry
* Prompt for if you are struggling to know what to write: **What is a weakness of yours and how could you improve it?**

Today I have:
Feel free to add your own examples
- [ ] exercised for 10 mins
- [ ] taken time to relax
- [ ] eaten well
- [ ] used my support network
- [ ] made my bed
- [ ] taken my medication
- [ ] connected with a friend
- [ ] disconnected from technology
- [ ]
- [ ]
- [ ]

Tonight I am anxious about:
* Do not feel obliged to fill in anything here. The purpose is to put on paper anything that is troubling you as you attempt to sleep, doing so can often move the mind away from that thought.

www.iam1in4.com — Reducing the stigma around mental health

Morning

Aim to complete the left hand page first thing in the morning, BEFORE you first check your phone or similar devices. Doing so helps to give you a solid base prior to the inevitable distractions of e-mail, social media, messages, news etc.

Approx how many hours did I sleep for?	How well rested am I? 1 = exhausted 6 = full of energy	Current Mood 1 = awful 6 = amazing

My priorities today are...

1.

2.

3.

* Reminder: No more than 3, keep them realistic and do not berate yourself if you don't always achieve all 3.

Today I am grateful for...

1.

2.

3.

* Reminder: These can be tiny, but try to not simply repeat the previous day's list

www.iam1in4.com   Find us on Facebook, Twitter & Instagram

Evening

The right hand page can be completed at a time in the day that suits you best.
However, it is recommended to make it part of your evening / bed time routine. By doing so you are able to put some of your concerns aside to help with a better night's sleep.

Journal Entry
Prompt for if you are struggling to know what to write: **What is your wildest dream?**

Today I have:
Feel free to add your own examples
- [ ] exercised for 10 mins
- [ ] taken time to relax
- [ ] eaten well
- [ ] used my support network
- [ ] made my bed
- [ ] taken my medication
- [ ] connected with a friend
- [ ] disconnected from technology
- [ ]
- [ ]
- [ ]

Tonight I am anxious about:
Do not feel obliged to fill in anything here. The purpose is to put on paper anything that is troubling you as you attempt to sleep, doing so can often move the mind away from that thought.

www.iam1in4.com   Reducing the stigma around mental health

Morning

Aim to complete the left hand page first thing in the morning, BEFORE you first check your phone or similar devices. Doing so helps to give you a solid base prior to the inevitable distractions of e-mail, social media, messages, news etc.

Approx how many hours did I sleep for?	How well rested am I? 1 = exhausted 6 = full of energy	Current Mood 1 = awful 6 = amazing

My priorities today are...

1.

2.

3.

* Reminder: No more than 3, keep them realistic and do not berate yourself if you don't always achieve all 3.

Today I am grateful for...

1.

2.

3.

* Reminder: These can be tiny, but try to not simply repeat the previous day's list

www.iam1in4.com   Find us on Facebook, Twitter & Instagram

Evening

The right hand page can be completed at a time in the day that suits you best.
However, it is recommended to make it part of your evening / bed time routine. By doing so you are able to put some of your concerns aside to help with a better night's sleep.

Journal Entry
* Prompt for if you are struggling to know what to write: **Who was your favourite teacher, and why?**

Today I have:
Feel free to add your own examples
- [ ] exercised for 10 mins
- [ ] taken time to relax
- [ ] eaten well
- [ ] used my support network
- [ ] made my bed
- [ ] taken my medication
- [ ] connected with a friend
- [ ] disconnected from technology
- [ ]
- [ ]
- [ ]

Tonight I am anxious about:
* Do not feel obliged to fill in anything here. The purpose is to put on paper anything that is troubling you as you attempt to sleep, doing so can often move the mind away from that thought.

Morning

Aim to complete the left hand page first thing in the morning, BEFORE you first check your phone or similar devices. Doing so helps to give you a solid base prior to the inevitable distractions of e-mail, social media, messages, news etc.

Approx how many hours did I sleep for?	How well rested am I? 1 = exhausted 6 = full of energy	Current Mood 1 = awful 6 = amazing

My priorities today are...

1.

2.

3.

* Reminder: No more than 3, keep them realistic and do not berate yourself if you don't always achieve all 3.

Today I am grateful for...

1.

2.

3.

* Reminder: These can be tiny, but try to not simply repeat the previous day's list

www.iam1in4.com   Find us on Facebook, Twitter & Instagram

Evening

The right hand page can be completed at a time in the day that suits you best.
However, it is recommended to make it part of your evening / bed time routine. By doing so you are able to put some of your concerns aside to help with a better night's sleep.

Journal Entry
* Prompt for if you are struggling to know what to write: **What book have your read over and over again, and why?**

Today I have:
Feel free to add your own examples
[ ] exercised for 10 mins
[ ] taken time to relax
[ ] eaten well
[ ] used my support network
[ ] made my bed
[ ] taken my medication
[ ] connected with a friend
[ ] disconnected from technology
[ ]
[ ]
[ ]

Tonight I am anxious about:
* Do not feel obliged to fill in anything here. The purpose is to put on paper anything that is troubling you as you attempt to sleep, doing so can often move the mind away from that thought.

www.iam1in4.com   Reducing the stigma around mental health

Morning

Aim to complete the left hand page first thing in the morning, BEFORE you first check your phone or similar devices. Doing so helps to give you a solid base prior to the inevitable distractions of e-mail, social media, messages, news etc.

Approx how many hours did I sleep for?	How well rested am I? 1 = exhausted 6 = full of energy	Current Mood 1 = awful 6 = amazing

My priorities today are...

1.

2.

3.

* Reminder: No more than 3, keep them realistic and do not berate yourself if you don't always achieve all 3.

Today I am grateful for...

1.

2.

3.

* Reminder: These can be tiny, but try to not simply repeat the previous day's list

www.iam1in4.com Find us on Facebook, Twitter & Instagram

Evening

The right hand page can be completed at a time in the day that suits you best.
However, it is recommended to make it part of your evening / bed time routine. By doing so you are able to put some of your concerns aside to help with a better night's sleep.

Journal Entry
* Prompt for if you are struggling to know what to write: **What is one problem you want to overcome this week and how would you do so?**

Today I have:
Feel free to add your own examples

[ ] exercised for 10 mins
[ ] taken time to relax
[ ] eaten well
[ ] used my support network
[ ] made my bed
[ ] taken my medication
[ ] connected with a friend
[ ] disconnected from technology
[ ]
[ ]
[ ]

Tonight I am anxious about:
* Do not feel obliged to fill in anything here. The purpose is to put on paper anything that is troubling you as you attempt to sleep, doing so can often move the mind away from that thought.

www.iam1in4.com   Reducing the stigma around mental health

Morning

Aim to complete the left hand page first thing in the morning, BEFORE you first check your phone or similar devices. Doing so helps to give you a solid base prior to the inevitable distractions of e-mail, social media, messages, news etc.

Approx how many hours did I sleep for?	How well rested am I? 1 = exhausted 6 = full of energy	Current Mood 1 = awful 6 = amazing

My priorities today are...

1.

2.

3.

* Reminder: No more than 3, keep them realistic and do not berate yourself if you don't always achieve all 3.

Today I am grateful for...

1.

2.

3.

* Reminder: These can be tiny, but try to not simply repeat the previous day's list

www.iam1in4.com   Find us on Facebook, Twitter & Instagram

Evening

The right hand page can be completed at a time in the day that suits you best.
However, it is recommended to make it part of your evening / bed time routine. By doing so you are able to put some of your concerns aside to help with a better night's sleep.

Journal Entry
* Prompt for if you are struggling to know what to write: **What activities do you want to do more of?**

Today I have:
Feel free to add your own examples
- [ ] exercised for 10 mins
- [ ] taken time to relax
- [ ] eaten well
- [ ] used my support network
- [ ] made my bed
- [ ] taken my medication
- [ ] connected with a friend
- [ ] disconnected from technology
- [ ]
- [ ]
- [ ]

Tonight I am anxious about:
* Do not feel obliged to fill in anything here. The purpose is to put on paper anything that is troubling you as you attempt to sleep, doing so can often move the mind away from that thought.

Morning

Aim to complete the left hand page first thing in the morning, BEFORE you first check your phone or similar devices. Doing so helps to give you a solid base prior to the inevitable distractions of e-mail, social media, messages, news etc.

Approx how many hours did I sleep for?	How well rested am I? 1 = exhausted 6 = full of energy	Current Mood 1 = awful 6 = amazing

My priorities today are...

1.

2.

3.

*Reminder: No more than 3, keep them realistic and do not berate yourself if you don't always achieve all 3.

Today I am grateful for...

1.

2.

3.

*Reminder: These can be tiny, but try to not simply repeat the previous day's list

www.iam1in4.com　　　　　　　　　　　Find us on Facebook, Twitter & Instagram

Evening

The right hand page can be completed at a time in the day that suits you best.
However, it is recommended to make it part of your evening / bed time routine. By doing so you are able to put some of your concerns aside to help with a better night's sleep.

Journal Entry
* Prompt for if you are struggling to know what to write: **What was the most surprising thing to have happened this week?**

Today I have:
Feel free to add your own examples
[ ] exercised for 10 mins
[ ] taken time to relax
[ ] eaten well
[ ] used my support network
[ ] made my bed
[ ] taken my medication
[ ] connected with a friend
[ ] disconnected from technology
[ ]
[ ]
[ ]

Tonight I am anxious about:
* Do not feel obliged to fill in anything here. The purpose is to put on paper anything that is troubling you as you attempt to sleep, doing so can often move the mind away from that thought.

www.iam1in4.com   Reducing the stigma around mental health

Morning

Aim to complete the left hand page first thing in the morning, BEFORE you first check your phone or similar devices. Doing so helps to give you a solid base prior to the inevitable distractions of e-mail, social media, messages, news etc.

Approx how many hours did I sleep for?	How well rested am I? 1 = exhausted 6 = full of energy	Current Mood 1 = awful 6 = amazing

My priorities today are...

1.

2.

3.

* Reminder: No more than 3, keep them realistic and do not berate yourself if you don't always achieve all 3.

Today I am grateful for...

1.

2.

3.

* Reminder: These can be tiny, but try to not simply repeat the previous day's list

www.iam1in4.com   Find us on Facebook, Twitter & Instagram

Evening

The right hand page can be completed at a time in the day that suits you best.
However, it is recommended to make it part of your evening / bed time routine. By doing so you are able to put some of your concerns aside to help with a better night's sleep.

Journal Entry
*Prompt for if you are struggling to know what to write: "The most vulnerable I have ever felt was when I ..."

Today I have:
Feel free to add your own examples
[ ] exercised for 10 mins
[ ] taken time to relax
[ ] eaten well
[ ] used my support network
[ ] made my bed
[ ] taken my medication
[ ] connected with a friend
[ ] disconnected from technology
[ ]
[ ]
[ ]

Tonight I am anxious about:
*Do not feel obliged to fill in anything here. The purpose is to put on paper anything that is troubling you as you attempt to sleep, doing so can often move the mind away from that thought.

www.iam1in4.com   Reducing the stigma around mental health

Morning

Aim to complete the left hand page first thing in the morning, BEFORE you first check your phone or similar devices. Doing so helps to give you a solid base prior to the inevitable distractions of e-mail, social media, messages, news etc.

Approx how many hours did I sleep for?	How well rested am I? 1 = exhausted 6 = full of energy	Current Mood 1 = awful 6 = amazing

My priorities today are...

1.

2.

3.

* Reminder: No more than 3, keep them realistic and do not berate yourself if you don't always achieve all 3.

Today I am grateful for...

1.

2.

3.

* Reminder: These can be tiny, but try to not simply repeat the previous day's list

www.iam1in4.com   Find us on Facebook, Twitter & Instagram

Evening

The right hand page can be completed at a time in the day that suits you best.
However, it is recommended to make it part of your evening / bed time routine. By doing so you are able to put some of your concerns aside to help with a better night's sleep.

Journal Entry
* Prompt for if you are struggling to know what to write: **What is your secret desire?**

Today I have:
Feel free to add your own examples

[ ] exercised for 10 mins
[ ] taken time to relax
[ ] eaten well
[ ] used my support network
[ ] made my bed
[ ] taken my medication
[ ] connected with a friend
[ ] disconnected from technology
[ ]
[ ]
[ ]

Tonight I am anxious about:
* Do not feel obliged to fill in anything here. The purpose is to put on paper anything that is troubling you as you attempt to sleep, doing so can often move the mind away from that thought.

www.iam1in4.com   Reducing the stigma around mental health

Morning

Aim to complete the left hand page first thing in the morning, BEFORE you first check your phone or similar devices. Doing so helps to give you a solid base prior to the inevitable distractions of e-mail, social media, messages, news etc.

Approx how many hours did I sleep for?	How well rested am I? 1 = exhausted 6 = full of energy	Current Mood 1 = awful 6 = amazing

My priorities today are...

1.

2.

3.

* Reminder: No more than 3, keep them realistic and do not berate yourself if you don't always achieve all 3.

Today I am grateful for...

1.

2.

3.

* Reminder: These can be tiny, but try to not simply repeat the previous day's list

www.iam1in4.com   Find us on Facebook, Twitter & Instagram

Evening

The right hand page can be completed at a time in the day that suits you best.
However, it is recommended to make it part of your evening / bed time routine. By doing so you are able to put some of your concerns aside to help with a better night's sleep.

Journal Entry
* Prompt for if you are struggling to know what to write: Who do you feel the closest connection to and why?

Today I have:
Feel free to add your own examples
[ ] exercised for 10 mins
[ ] taken time to relax
[ ] eaten well
[ ] used my support network
[ ] made my bed
[ ] taken my medication
[ ] connected with a friend
[ ] disconnected from technology
[ ]
[ ]
[ ]

Tonight I am anxious about:
* Do not feel obliged to fill in anything here. The purpose is to put on paper anything that is troubling you as you attempt to sleep, doing so can often move the mind away from that thought.

Morning

Aim to complete the left hand page first thing in the morning, BEFORE you first check your phone or similar devices. Doing so helps to give you a solid base prior to the inevitable distractions of e-mail, social media, messages, news etc.

Approx how many hours did I sleep for?	How well rested am I? 1 = exhausted 6 = full of energy	Current Mood 1 = awful 6 = amazing

My priorities today are...

1.

2.

3.

* Reminder: No more than 3, keep them realistic and do not berate yourself if you don't always achieve all 3.

Today I am grateful for...

1.

2.

3.

* Reminder: These can be tiny, but try to not simply repeat the previous day's list

www.iam1in4.com   Find us on Facebook, Twitter & Instagram

Evening

The right hand page can be completed at a time in the day that suits you best.
However, it is recommended to make it part of your evening / bed time routine. By doing so you are able to put some of your concerns aside to help with a better night's sleep.

Journal Entry
* Prompt for if you are struggling to know what to write: **What is one hobbie you want to take up and why?**

Today I have:
Feel free to add your own examples
[ ] exercised for 10 mins
[ ] taken time to relax
[ ] eaten well
[ ] used my support network
[ ] made my bed
[ ] taken my medication
[ ] connected with a friend
[ ] disconnected from technology
[ ]
[ ]
[ ]

Tonight I am anxious about:
* Do not feel obliged to fill in anything here. The purpose is to put on paper anything that is troubling you as you attempt to sleep, doing so can often move the mind away from that thought.

www.iam1in4.com — Reducing the stigma around mental health

Morning

Aim to complete the left hand page first thing in the morning, BEFORE you first check your phone or similar devices. Doing so helps to give you a solid base prior to the inevitable distractions of e-mail, social media, messages, news etc.

Approx how many hours did I sleep for?	How well rested am I? 1 = exhausted 6 = full of energy	Current Mood 1 = awful 6 = amazing

My priorities today are...

1.

2.

3.

* Reminder: No more than 3, keep them realistic and do not berate yourself if you don't always achieve all 3.

Today I am grateful for...

1.

2.

3.

* Reminder: These can be tiny, but try to not simply repeat the previous day's list

www.iam1in4.com   Find us on Facebook, Twitter & Instagram

Evening

The right hand page can be completed at a time in the day that suits you best. However, it is recommended to make it part of your evening / bed time routine. By doing so you are able to put some of your concerns aside to help with a better night's sleep.

Journal Entry
* Prompt for if you are struggling to know what to write: **Do you believe in soul mates?**

Today I have:
Feel free to add your own examples
- [ ] exercised for 10 mins
- [ ] taken time to relax
- [ ] eaten well
- [ ] used my support network
- [ ] made my bed
- [ ] taken my medication
- [ ] connected with a friend
- [ ] disconnected from technology
- [ ]
- [ ]
- [ ]

Tonight I am anxious about:
* Do not feel obliged to fill in anything here. The purpose is to put on paper anything that is troubling you as you attempt to sleep, doing so can often move the mind away from that thought.

www.iam1in4.com   Reducing the stigma around mental health

Morning

Aim to complete the left hand page first thing in the morning, BEFORE you first check your phone or similar devices. Doing so helps to give you a solid base prior to the inevitable distractions of e-mail, social media, messages, news etc.

Approx how many hours did I sleep for?	How well rested am I? 1 = exhausted 6 = full of energy	Current Mood 1 = awful 6 = amazing

My priorities today are...

1.

2.

3.

* Reminder: No more than 3, keep them realistic and do not berate yourself if you don't always achieve all 3.

Today I am grateful for...

1.

2.

3.

* Reminder: These can be tiny, but try to not simply repeat the previous day's list

www.iam1in4.com Find us on Facebook, Twitter & Instagram

Evening

The right hand page can be completed at a time in the day that suits you best.
However, it is recommended to make it part of your evening / bed time routine. By doing so you are able to put some of your concerns aside to help with a better night's sleep.

Journal Entry
* Prompt for if you are struggling to know what to write: **What was the most outrageous thing you've ever done?**

Today I have:
Feel free to add your own examples
[ ] exercised for 10 mins
[ ] taken time to relax
[ ] eaten well
[ ] used my support network
[ ] made my bed
[ ] taken my medication
[ ] connected with a friend
[ ] disconnected from technology
[ ]
[ ]
[ ]

Tonight I am anxious about:
* Do not feel obliged to fill in anything here. The purpose is to put on paper anything that is troubling you as you attempt to sleep, doing so can often move the mind away from that thought.

www.iam1in4.com   Reducing the stigma around mental health

Morning

Aim to complete the left hand page first thing in the morning, BEFORE you first check your phone or similar devices. Doing so helps to give you a solid base prior to the inevitable distractions of e-mail, social media, messages, news etc.

Approx how many hours did I sleep for?	How well rested am I? 1 = exhausted 6 = full of energy	Current Mood 1 = awful 6 = amazing

My priorities today are...

1.

2.

3.

* Reminder: No more than 3, keep them realistic and do not berate yourself if you don't always achieve all 3.

Today I am grateful for...

1.

2.

3.

* Reminder: These can be tiny, but try to not simply repeat the previous day's list

www.iam1in4.com   Find us on Facebook, Twitter & Instagram

Evening

The right hand page can be completed at a time in the day that suits you best.
However, it is recommended to make it part of your evening / bed time routine. By doing so you are able to put some of your concerns aside to help with a better night's sleep.

Journal Entry
* Prompt for if you are struggling to know what to write: **What do you look forward to the most?**

Today I have:
Feel free to add your own examples
[ ] exercised for 10 mins
[ ] taken time to relax
[ ] eaten well
[ ] used my support network
[ ] made my bed
[ ] taken my medication
[ ] connected with a friend
[ ] disconnected from technology
[ ]
[ ]
[ ]

Tonight I am anxious about:
* Do not feel obliged to fill in anything here. The purpose is to put on paper anything that is troubling you as you attempt to sleep, doing so can often move the mind away from that thought.

www.iam1in4.com   Reducing the stigma around mental health

Morning

Aim to complete the left hand page first thing in the morning, BEFORE you first check your phone or similar devices. Doing so helps to give you a solid base prior to the inevitable distractions of e-mail, social media, messages, news etc.

Approx how many hours did I sleep for?	How well rested am I? 1 = exhausted 6 = full of energy	Current Mood 1 = awful 6 = amazing

My priorities today are...

1.

2.

3.

* Reminder: No more than 3, keep them realistic and do not berate yourself if you don't always achieve all 3.

Today I am grateful for...

1.

2.

3.

* Reminder: These can be tiny, but try to not simply repeat the previous day's list

www.iam1in4.com   Find us on Facebook, Twitter & Instagram

Evening

The right hand page can be completed at a time in the day that suits you best.
However, it is recommended to make it part of your evening / bed time routine. By doing so you are able to put some of your concerns aside to help with a better night's sleep.

Journal Entry
* Prompt for if you are struggling to know what to write: **What do you admire most about one of your closest friends?**

Today I have:
Feel free to add your own examples
[ ] exercised for 10 mins
[ ] taken time to relax
[ ] eaten well
[ ] used my support network
[ ] made my bed
[ ] taken my medication
[ ] connected with a friend
[ ] disconnected from technology
[ ]
[ ]
[ ]

Tonight I am anxious about:
* Do not feel obliged to fill in anything here. The purpose is to put on paper anything that is troubling you as you attempt to sleep, doing so can often move the mind away from that thought.

Morning

Aim to complete the left hand page first thing in the morning, BEFORE you first check your phone or similar devices. Doing so helps to give you a solid base prior to the inevitable distractions of e-mail, social media, messages, news etc.

Approx how many hours did I sleep for?	How well rested am I? 1 = exhausted 6 = full of energy	Current Mood 1 = awful 6 = amazing

My priorities today are...

1.

2.

3.

* Reminder: No more than 3, keep them realistic and do not berate yourself if you don't always achieve all 3.

Today I am grateful for...

1.

2.

3.

* Reminder: These can be tiny, but try to not simply repeat the previous day's list

www.iam1in4.com   Find us on Facebook, Twitter & Instagram

Evening

The right hand page can be completed at a time in the day that suits you best.
However, it is recommended to make it part of your evening / bed time routine. By doing so you are able to put some of your concerns aside to help with a better night's sleep.

Journal Entry
* Prompt for if you are struggling to know what to write: **How have you been feeling this week?**

Today I have:
Feel free to add your own examples
[ ] exercised for 10 mins
[ ] taken time to relax
[ ] eaten well
[ ] used my support network
[ ] made my bed
[ ] taken my medication
[ ] connected with a friend
[ ] disconnected from technology
[ ]
[ ]
[ ]

Tonight I am anxious about:
* Do not feel obliged to fill in anything here. The purpose is to put on paper anything that is troubling you as you attempt to sleep, doing so can often move the mind away from that thought.

Made in the USA
Middletown, DE
20 January 2019